LESSONS FROM THE BACK PEW

by

Tim Searcy

God Bless You!
Ephesians 2:8-9
De Colores!
Michelle Seay

Printed in the United States of America

First Printing, 2018

ISBN-13: 978-0692068557
ISBN-10: 0692068554

Catalyst Solutions Publishing
9648 North Box Elder Court
McCordsville, Indiana 46055

CONTENTS

LESSONS FROM THE BACK PEW

Acknowledgements

This whole thing is Jason Duff's fault and he knows why!
If he had not been prompted by God many years ago to tell me I
should think about writing a faith book, I may never have gotten
started. However, He listens to God, and I listened to him, and
so now here we are!

The last 10 years of my faith journey have been
remarkable, and without pastors at Holy Cross Lutheran Church
like John Sattler, Terry Hursh, and Dave McClean, much of the
lessons from the back pew would never have formed. Likewise,
the Trinity Great Banquet and Kairos Communities have
supported me and involved me in many retreat and speaking
opportunities, which forced me to truly examine for the first
time, the real issues of grace and forgiveness and agape love.

I have been blessed by a Men's Bible study that meets a couple of times per month and has for almost 20 years of my life in Indianapolis. These men are strong in faith, biting in commentary, and loving and generous to everyone. It is their example that encouraged me to step out on a limb and write some things down related to grace.

My family has been a never-ending source of spiritual and personal inspiration, and from the daily devotion that my parents read out loud to us as children through their openness about their own journeys, my parents have never drifted from their Biblical duties to raise their children to be God fearing and God loving. My life is possible and rich because of them. My daughter and son, my wife's family, and my siblings and their families have been unbelievable in their encouragement and willingness to patiently listen to me talk about ideas. They have been willing to read drafts of chapters or beginning of ideas and have been honest and clear in their feedback. It has been wonderful, and I could not ask for more.

My brother Tom is truly the writer in the family, and his advice, editing, encouragement and critical eye have made this process into something worthwhile as opposed to a project at the back of my desk. His time and diligence on this project are humbling, and I am so very grateful for him every day.

Finally, my wife deserves more thanks than anyone. It is through her prayers that I returned to faith, it is through her example that I became interested again in the Word, and it is through her unfailing love that I began to see what God's grace looks like when shared by a human being. Michelle is the very best of the person I would like to become, and I thank God for her every hour of every day.

LESSONS FROM THE BACK PEW

Chapter 1: Grace Is Served

"Who shall separate us from the love of Christ? Shall tribulation, or distress, or persecution, or famine, or nakedness, or danger, or sword? As it is written,

> "For your sake we are being killed all day long;
> we are regarded as sheep to be slaughtered."

No, in all these things we are more than conquerors through him who loved us. For I am sure that neither death nor life, nor angels nor rulers, nor things present nor things to come, nor powers, nor height nor depth, nor anything else in all creation, will be able to separate us from the love of God in Christ Jesus our Lord."

Romans 8:35-39 (ESV)

I would have put the contents below in the Introduction, but so often, people refuse to read introductions, and then where would we be? I mean really, if a writer has a point to make, they should make it right away so that if you are reading the book in the bookstore, and you don't like the point, you don't waste your money on the whole book. Publishers however, are forever encouraging authors to 'bury the lead' a little bit so that people have to read for a while, and that lures the customer by creating just enough curiosity at the bookstore to make the purchase. I could be wrong, but I suspect that this has something to do with money.

Let me be clear, this whole book . . . every syllable of it is about God's grace and the not so silly things that we let get in the way of it. Why write about grace and the obstacles to accepting it? God didn't even tell me this was going to be about grace for a few months while I was writing this book. Here is what struck me after I had written a few of the chapters . . . the whole thing was tied together by the concept that grace is freely given, and we unknowingly let Satan try to snatch it out of our hands and hearts because we don't recognize it, accept it and very importantly, give it to others.

We are called to <u>freely accept</u> God's gift of grace.

I was on a retreat with a bunch of men, and the concept of grace came up the entire time. Questions about grace faced me throughout our sessions: "What is it? No, what is it really? No, I mean it, help me pin it down a little more. What do I have to do to get it? How will I know I have it? What do I do to get more of it? Can I lose it?" It was a little unnerving to spend so much time on a topic that, technically speaking, is as simple as walking and breathing. That's the conundrum: Grace is too simple and too powerful to be true! I did not say grace was cheap, or easy, but as an idea it is simple.

"But God, being rich in mercy, because of the great love with which he loved us, even when we were dead in our trespasses, made us alive together with Christ—by grace you have been saved— and raised us up with him and seated us with him in the heavenly places in Christ Jesus, so that in the coming ages he might show the immeasurable riches of his grace in kindness toward us in Christ Jesus. For by grace you have been saved through faith. And this is not your own doing; it is the gift of God, not a result of works, so that no one may boast."

Ephesians 2:4-9 (ESV)

All the definitions of grace that I have read point to an unearned, unmerited, and undeserved overflowing measure of God's love and forgiveness of us. These are expressed through the death and resurrection of his Son, Jesus on the cross. It is personal and collective insomuch as Jesus would have died for just one of us, but indeed died for all that have been, were in His time, and were to come until the end of time. Grace is a gift from God that cannot be repaid because nothing is equal to the sacrifice made to give it to us. Grace is what gets believers to be able, even in our imperfection, to live forever in heaven with a perfect Triune God. Maybe I was wrong before. Maybe grace isn't really that simple.

As a life redeemed, grace is nearly impossible for me to accept, which is where the problem comes in. The lack of selfishness is what humbles us. We did nothing to earn it. We can do nothing to keep it. And we can do nothing to get more of it. It is a gift, freely given, and hard fought for by an individual we have never shaken hands with. . . Jesus. The more we are confronted with the sinfulness of our lives, the more improbable to our minds that we would be eligible to receive it. We are so consumed by the notion of quid pro quo, or an exchange of things that have similar or equal value, that a one-sided deal makes our heads rattle. This grace thing seems cheap only because we did not pay for it.

During the Men's retreat weekend, a three-phrase concept was introduced that helped me a little bit:

- <u>Justice is getting what we deserve.</u> This actually makes some sense. We all cheer for justice for other people. Someone commits a crime, and we want them punished and for the victim to receive the satisfaction of justice. If we were to get what we deserve as sinners, we would simply die and ultimately go to hell. We will cover it more later, but the Bible says in Romans 6:23 (ESV), "The wages of sin are death."

- <u>Mercy is not getting what we deserve.</u> When a policeman lets us off with a warning instead of getting a ticket, we have received mercy. When a child receives no punishment for a wrong they have done, you have given them mercy. Mercy is not necessarily a good teacher, and it replaces consequences with sympathy, but we all want it. It is very rare that someone will knowingly choose to not accept mercy.

- <u>Grace is getting what we do not deserve.</u> This is doing something horrible, and then the people you wronged handing you a million dollars. It is the exact opposite of what we should receive. When Jesus died for our sins, and opened the gates of heaven for those that believe in Him, He gave us grace. We do not deserve forgiveness or eternity with Him, but here we are!

I am a list guy. I make lists for everything, and I derive great pleasure from checking boxes on my list. Even working through big ideas requires a list for me. Here is a checklist:

- I am sinful. Check . . . I get that.
- I am unworthy of God's love and forgiveness because though I may repent, I will sin again and again. Check, I get that one too.
- My sin has separated me from God. Check and Double Check, because I certainly don't always feel close to God, and I am pretty sure it is more about me than Him. Oh, this is a major check!
- I cannot close the gap between myself and God due to the chasm of sin that I continue to create. (Still checking boxes confidently!)

- I need a savior, because this doing it on my own thing is not really working. My list of things I understand and accept is nearly complete.

- Jesus Christ was that Savior. This is the only check I really need, but the earlier ones seem to be what I think about. If I got this one, I have all I need. Jesus said, "I am the way, and the truth and the life. No one comes to the Father except through me." – John 14:6 (ESV)

- If Jesus has given me grace and won for me eternal life, I should share that message with everyone I meet so that they can have it too. Jesus did not do this just for me, although He would have, He did if for everyone. Whoa! Hold on! When the boxes were filling with check marks that made my life better, I was a big fan; but now that it involves sharing with others, my pen is shaking over my list and this last box is at great risk of going unchecked!

Grace is so much better than justice or mercy! But the concept of it is overwhelming because it is like hitting a lottery that you never bought a ticket for! You literally did nothing to earn it, and yet there it sits smack dab in the middle of your eternal life as a central theme. This is so straightforward, most of us that come to understand it think we must be cheating to have it so good! We have all the answers to the only test that ever mattered, and not only can we share the answers, we are asked to! I love the way this school operates!

"For sin will have no dominion over you, since you are not under law but under *grace*."

Romans 6:14 (ESV)

The weight of grace is not in the receipt, but in paying it forward. When a king is crowned in succession, he has done nothing to earn his kingdom except be born into the right family. However, from that day forward, for good or bad, his decisions will impact all in his kingdom. If he is to be a good king, he must accept what is referred to as "noblesse oblige," or in English, the obligation of nobility. When we received the crown of righteousness through grace, we also received a similar obligation of nobility; but rather than duty, it becomes desire. Once you have experienced grace, selfishness with this amazing gift becomes increasingly difficult. Sharing this gift in the form of our living example, humility, forgiveness, generosity and the fruits of the spirit, becomes our heartfelt interest.

Of course, if we were not human, this wonderful sense of love, joy and generosity in grace would overwhelm our own sinful nature, and happiness would run rampant everywhere! Unfortunately, we let most things get in the way of sharing this special gift called grace. In the rest of this book, I will share what has gotten in my way. We will look at the hang ups, judgments, fear, willfulness, and laziness that have kept me from sharing God's grace with people in my life and sharing the message of God's grace with everyone. It is my hope that from my brokenness and foolishness, the Holy Spirit will lead you to experience, give and share grace with others.

One element that I have often overlooked in the concept of grace is that the gift is self-sustaining. When we speak of sustainable energy, the concept is really about energy sources that never run out or exhaust. Sometimes these are referred to as renewable sources of energy. Grace is the ultimate renewable energy source because it is from God, it never runs out! What does this mean from a practical standpoint? It means that God will never let you run out of the grace necessary to share grace! The gift is so powerful that you can give it all away, and still keep all of it for yourself. It is the ultimate flywheel, the quintessential perpetual motion device, and only our choice can slow it down or cause the receiving of it to stop. I pray that this book resonates with you and that you move forward in confidence, love and most importantly, the knowledge and acceptance of God's grace.

Chapter 1 Summary

Key Points:

- Grace is freely given by God.
- Grace is getting what we don't deserve, which is different than justice or mercy.
- Once the gift is received, it is a natural condition of our new life to want to share this gift with others.
- Our sinful nature, circumstance, and Satan work diligently to keep us from sharing this gift.
- Part of the gift's strength is found in the relationship with God, which helps us overcome the obstacles to sharing grace.

Key Questions:

- Do you truly feel the grace you have been given? Do you know its weight and value?
- How do experience grace in your life now?
- Do you give grace to others in the form of responding differently than people deserve?
- Have you cheapened the grace you are to give by replacing it with mercy?

- How do you think the Grace Giver feels about His unrequited Grace?

Prayer:

Lord, thank you for eyes to see and read, and a mouth to share your grace with others. As I begin to read this book, help me identify how your grace blesses my life every day, and show me opportunities to share your love and grace with those around me. Please remove the obstacles in my life that keep me from experiencing the wonder of your grace completely. I ask these things in your Son's name. Amen.

Chapter 2: My Love Is Unconditional

"Love is patient and kind; love does not envy or boast; it is not arrogant or rude. It does not insist on its own way; it is not irritable or resentful; it does not rejoice at wrongdoing but rejoices with the truth. Love bears all things, believes all things, hopes all things, endures all things."

1 Corinthians 13:4-7 (ESV)

My wife and I were fortunate enough to have the means to cover the expenses for college for our two children. This was a gift we wanted to give our children, but it did not come without strings attached. When each of our children went to college, we had them sign a contract. The first paragraph of the contract opened with, "Our love for you is unconditional, but our financial support of your college education is completely conditional." We wanted to make certain they understood our love operated without conditions, but our day-to-day relationship had expectations and consequences.

Love is a word so misused and over abused that it has lost a lot of its meaning. You can't listen to a pop song, read a new book, or hardly enter into a conversation that love does not come up. Love has become a meme for any strong positive emotion we have towards anyone or anything. It gets a little ridiculous. When we truly understand the definition of love as God sees it, we see that people make foolish use of an all-encompassing thought. And as we will discuss throughout this book, "people" *always* includes you and me.

Conditional love is an obstacle to accepting grace.

It is not popular in modern culture to place <u>stated</u> conditions on relationships. However, conditions of acceptance often exist, whether they are in the open or held in our hearts and minds. Because love is such a deep emotion, our conditions for it may be the most profound. If our love has been rejected in the past, we may be brittle about it, and therefore only willing to accept and return love when very strict conditions are met. If our love has been taken for granted or abused, we see ourselves as incapable of love without restrictions and guidelines. All people have been disappointed in a love relationship at some point in time or another. The only perfect love relationship that can exist is with God, and all other love relationships are destined for difficulty.

> "Stop trusting in mere humans,
>
> who have but a breath in their nostrils.
>
> Why hold them in esteem?"
>
> **Isaiah 2:22 (NIV)**

In response to our history with love, whether we like it or not, we put conditions on our love in the form of "until" statements.

Examples of "until" restrictions on love include things like:

- I will love you until someone better comes along.
- I will love you until you break my heart.
- I will love you until I fall out of love with you due to time or a change of interests.

More examples of "until" restrictions on love are often the opposite of the marriage vows which have been popularized on television and movies:

- I will love you until you run out of money or money-making prospects.
- I will love you until you become sick.
- I will love you until the good times become bad times.
- I will love you until you have done me wrong, or wrongs have piled up to a certain height.
- I will love you until I can't forgive you any more.
- I will love you until I can't forgive myself any more.
- I will love you until my faithfulness to you, or your faithfulness to me, comes into question.

These samples of until statements are not just reserved for the marriage or love relationship between a man and a woman. In their way they apply to our parents, friends, church members and people we come in contact with. Many of the closest relationships we have had became estranged because someone crossed over that "until" limit, and we decided we could not love them anymore.

The opposite type of statement is also true. We place conditions on new relationships that start with, "I will not love you until . . . "

- I will not love you until I am 100% certain that you love me first.
- I will not love you until I have determined that you are worthy of my love.
- I will not love you until I know that you are acceptable to the people I care about.
- I will not love you until I am no longer scared of what truly loving you would mean.
- I will not love you until you sacrifice certain parts of who you are (the parts I do not like) so you can become more lovable to me.

We are born to love, and we are born to be around others that we love and in turn love us. We choose to be around people we love. We make time for them, and we seek them out regularly. Our lives revolve around the people we love, and we seek ways to increase that love through time, conversation and emotional exchange.

"Now that you have purified yourselves by obeying the truth so that you have sincere love for each other, love one another deeply, from the heart."

1 Peter 1:22 (NIV)

Living without the capacity to love someone is misery. We trade our acceptance of people's sinful or foolish ways, as part of who they are, for a lack of acceptance; and therefore distance of ourselves from them. Conversely, those that we no longer love become painful to see or hear about. Our lack of love can quickly turn to anger or bitterness. We harden our hearts to them for fear that love might find its way in and we risk again being hurt. The fear of a repeat of that cycle saps energy for positive enjoyment, and removes our willingness to seek a loving relationship with others.

God's love for me is unconditional. That is great! He has no "until" restrictions on His love because He knows that if He did that, we would never be able to live up to the standard. If He said, "I will love you until you take my name in vain, or until you put something before my relationship with you, or until you forget about me," He could not love any of us. God is incapable of living in misery, so He does not impose the conditional nature of love that we use. By operating without expectations on your love relationships, you become free to love like God.

Now, as overworked and misused as the word love may be, I think people use the word "like," much more consistently. My like for people is completely conditional. Like is a word I can work with! Like and dislike are safe and friendly words and they are easy to manipulate. We have "Like" and now "Dislike," in all of our social media. We are reinforced on applications like Pandora and Facebook to select one of these responses so that they can further refine what we see and hear to be more about what we like. In essence, technology is working to carefully remove those things that create negative reactions in us. Thanks technology . . .I guess.

Why do we like people? Liking people comes down to understanding something about ourselves. We like people for one of two reasons; because they are similar to us, or they have traits that we wish we possessed. We like people that we feel we understand and can accept. If you ask someone to describe the people they like, you will find an echo of themselves in the narrative. It is small irony that if you ask someone to describe the people they don't like, you may hear an even louder echo in the narrative. It is fair to say that like and dislike of others starts with the feelings we have for the person in the mirror.

In fact, we do not like people; we accept and encourage behavior in people. If they behave as we want, then we smile, compliment, or express affection. If they behave in an undesirable way, we grimace, say something unkind, or show disapproval. In this way, we condition their behavior to what we want through our behavior in response to them. Our emotional status with these individuals is based primarily upon their willingness and ability to satisfy what we have deemed acceptable from them.

God is incapable of liking us. The concept of conditional behavior makes no sense to God in relationship to His creation. Certainly, He created a covenant relationship with his people that demanded certain conditions be met for the covenant to remain in place. But, God has always been faithful in His love for His creation.

As Christians, we are often reminded that we need to "love the sinner but hate the sin." Unfortunately, I find that concept a bit patronizing. It has a certain implied superiority, as though I am capable of being so wise as to separate the sin and sinner effectively and consistently. Sin and sinner are inseparable for God. Only His Son can remove the sin so that God can be in relationship with what was once a sinner. How does this work? God chooses to no longer remember our sins.

"I have blotted out *your* transgressions like a cloud

and *your* sins like mist; return to me, for I have redeemed

you."

Isaiah 44:22 (ESV)

"but God shows His love for us in

that *while we were still* sinners, Christ died for us."

Romans 5:8 (ESV)

What conditions has God placed upon us for His love? None!
How about His grace? None! Which conditions are fair for us to
employ when considering loving our neighbor? Same answer.
The causes for our conditions are irrelevant to God. You and I
may have very good reasons not to love someone. The line of
horrific acts and thoughts, both perceived and proven in truth,
from person to person have been cataloged throughout history.
If you think back on your own life, there are probably some
"unforgivable" things that people have done to you. As a matter
of fact, there is no condition, including their begging for
forgiveness, that will satisfy your standards to love them.   And
Jesus does not care. He clearly says to us to love one another,
and there are no ifs, ands or buts!

Chapter 2 Summary

Key Points:

- There is a clear definition of what love is, and what it is not, when we think about God.
- The concepts of love and like are separate in how we view our neighbors, how we treat them, and how we respond to their behavior toward us and others.
- Our demand of people that they be likable for us to love them is inconsistent with God's will for us.

Key Questions:

- How do you let the conditional thinking associated with "like" get in the way of your loving acceptance of God's grace?
- How do you let "likeability" get in your way of sharing grace with others?
- How do you set conditions on your willingness to like others; and if we are to be Jesus, why can you not set conditions on your love for them?

Prayer:

Abba (Father), you are love, and I know this. It is your love that was so unconditional that you sent your only Son to redeem me so that you and I would no longer be separated by my sin. I do not always like people, and I set conditions on my love that get in the way of relationships that you desire for me to have with you and others. Please help me to love others as you love me, to forgive others as you forgive me, and to treat others as you treat me. I ask this in your Son's name. Amen.

Chapter 3: We All Want to Get an A

"Whoever has my commandments and keeps them, he it is who loves me. And he who loves me will be loved by my Father, and I will love him and manifest myself to him."

John 14:21 (ESV)

"Doesn't live up to his potential," "Not completely engaged in class," and "Not giving his best effort," have all appeared on a report card several times in my life I am sure. As passionate as I am, the energy to get all the way to the finish line with my best efforts has often eluded me. I never finished college, and as a matter of fact, I would not say I have finished a lot of things in my life. Don't get me wrong, I am a great starter! But I get bored. The tedium of more of the same every day just catches up with me and drags me into a new direction where I can be a starter again. This short book that you hold in your hand was four years in the making (at least)! How about you? Do you have a hard time finishing things?

In my Junior year as a high school student, the Teacher of the Year was Alex Pritchard. Mr. Pritchard taught Economics, Psychology, and Debate. He was a great teacher with a very dry sense of humor and sarcasm that cut with laser like efficiency. He would start every year in school with the same speech, "You cannot get an "A" in this class unless I like you." He would proceed to make a list of the things that were necessary for him to like you. Like me, his like for each person was completely conditional on certain things. Doing homework, participating in class, getting the answers right on his test and showing up to class on time, every time, were his typical standards for liking you. If you did these things, you dramatically increased your chances to get an A.

My wife and I live in an upwardly mobile, upper middle-class community, on the upper East side, of our upper mid-west city. To say that we are uppity is probably to know us too well. I don't mean snobbish, just certain that our clothes are clean, our cars are newer, and our house is presentable. We don't look down on people, but we sure don't want to look up at them either. We proudly survive in the 3% of the population that is targeted for taxes and the derision by government folks just looking out for everyone's best interest.

In our uppity world, kids are supposed to get "A's" in school. As a matter of fact, my wife is the Administrator at a Lutheran School, and she will tell you that the lack of an A on a report card will cause parents to question everything from the teacher's sanity, to the fairness of age appropriate curriculum. Of course, these same parents will not inquire as to their child's attention level in class, homework completion or study habits, as these could not possibly be relevant. Anything that separates a child from an "A" is to be removed. The one certainty for achieving that grade is that it does not require parental supervision or more work for the child.

The need for achievement in a relationship with God gets in the way of His grace.

It dawned on me that we all want to get an "A" in our lives in whatever our pursuit. If it is work, we want promotions, raises and praise for outstanding performance. Society propels us to seek an "A" in the court of public opinion for our looks, fitness, conspicuous consumption and fashion sense. Even our children are a source of valuable grades showered upon us for their accomplishments. If we are all so driven to get "A's", why wouldn't we want to get top marks in our relationship with

God? It seems only fitting to want to get an average of 4.0 on the biggest report card we can ever imagine.

Please understand, God loves us whether we are an "A" student or an "F" student. His requirements for love are absolutely nothing. God does not keep score like people. We can do nothing to make God love us more or less. We cannot get more grace by doing things that are pleasing to God. However, our lives will improve immensely if we align to His will through understanding His word and living His commands.

All disclaimers and explanations aside, you might be asking the question implied by the chapter title, "How do I get an "A" with God?" In the movie Chariots of Fire, the main character Eric Liddell said, "I believe God made me for a purpose, but He also made me fast. And when I run I feel His pleasure." In the movie, this character used God's gifts to share the message of Jesus Christ. How does a runner make the leap from running to evangelism?

On the podium, this was Eric's acceptance speech: "You came to see a race today. To see some one win. It happened to be me. But I want you to do more than just watch a race. I want you to take part in it. I want to compare faith to running in a race. It's hard. It requires concentration of will, energy of soul. You experience elation when the winner breaks the tape - especially if you've got a bet on it. But how long does that last? You go home. Maybe you're dinner's burnt. Maybe you haven't got a job. So who am I to say, "Believe, have faith," in the face of life's realities? I would like to give you something more permanent, but I can only point the way. I have no formula for winning the race. Everyone runs in her own way, or his own way. And where does the power come from, to see the race to its end? From within. Jesus said, 'Behold, the Kingdom of God is within you. If with all your hearts, you truly seek me, you shall ever surely find me.' If you commit yourself to the love of Christ, then that is how you run a straight race."

I am more than a little jealous of Eric Liddell! I want to feel God's pleasure too! I want to feel the Lord's pleasure and see Him smile because I have done His will. Like Paul, I want to be able to say,

"I have fought the good fight, I have finished the race, I have kept the faith. Henceforth there is laid up for me the crown of righteousness, which the Lord, the righteous judge, will award to me on that day . . ."

2 Timothy 4:7-8 (ESV)

This is pride, and even if it is the hope of pride in serving God, I suspect that it is a sinful aspiration. I rationalize that pleasing God seems like a worthwhile pursuit. Who doesn't want to make their Father proud? Jesus declared His work before the Father, much as we wish we could,

"I have manifested your name to the people whom you gave me out of the world. Yours they were, and you gave them to me, and they have kept your word. Now they know that everything that you have given me is from you. For I have given them the words that you gave me, and they have received them and have come to know in truth that I came from you; and they have believed that you sent me. I am praying for them. I am not praying for the world but for those whom you have given me, for they are yours. All mine are yours, and yours are mine, and I am glorified in them."

John 17:6-10 (ESV)

Now before my Christian friends correctly point out the ideology conflict, I think I will do it for them. A logical point would be that a tenant of our faith is that God does the doing, and we are merely his vessels. Good theology would point out that we do nothing without the power of God.

"So Jesus said to them, 'Truly, truly, I say to you, the Son can do nothing of His own accord, but only what He sees the Father doing. For whatever the Father does, that the Son does likewise.'"

John 5:19 (ESV)

If Jesus can do nothing of His own accord, how much truer must this be of you and me? Let me make certain we are clear, any good works that we may accomplish only happen by the grace of God. However, we must be receptive to His will and willing to act upon His instructions. But are we clear enough on God's instructions to us?

I know that the use of BIBLE as an acronym has become popular, (Basic Instructions Before Leaving Earth). It even shows up in a rap song by Killah Priest. But as cool a concept as this is, it misses the important aspect of the instructions it provides for living on earth.   It is preferable to consider the Bible to be the instruction book for our life on earth.

We are aware of the two commandments that Jesus gave us:

> "You shall love the Lord your God with all your heart and with all your soul and with all your mind. This is the great and first commandment. And a second is like it: You shall love your neighbor as yourself. On these two commandments depend all the Law and the Prophets."
>
> **Matthew 22:37-40 (ESV)**

In addition to these commandments, Jesus also gave us other commandments which, although naturally derivative of the first two, give us more clarity. Jesus made it easier for us by giving us lessons in practical Christianity. Here are just 19 examples of Jesus' clear commandments to us from the gospel of Matthew (ESV). These are not guidelines or suggestions, but commandments for how we are to live.

1. **Repent:** *From that time Jesus began to preach, saying, "Repent, for the kingdom of heaven is at hand."* (Matthew 4:17).

2. **Follow Him:** *And He said to them, "Follow me, and I will make you fishers of men."* (Matthew 4:19).

3. **Rejoice in poor of your treatment by others because of me:** *"Blessed are you when others revile you and persecute you and utter all kinds of evil against you falsely on my account. Rejoice and be glad, for your reward is great in heaven, for so they persecuted the prophets who were before you."* (Matthew 5:11–12).

4. **Avoid letting conflict damage relationships:** *"So if you are offering your gift at the altar and there remember that your brother has something against you, leave your gift there before the altar and go. First be reconciled to your brother, and then come and offer your gift. Come to terms quickly with your accuser while you are going with him to court, lest your accuser hand you over to the judge, and the judge to the guard, and you be put in prison."* (Matthew 5:23–25).

5. **Do not let lust and desire lead you astray:** *"But I say to you that everyone who looks at a woman with lustful intent has already committed adultery with her in his heart. If your right eye causes you to sin, tear it out and throw it away. For it is better that you lose one of your members than that your whole body be thrown into hell.*

And if your right hand causes you to sin, cut it off and throw it away. For it is better that you lose one of your members than that your whole body go into hell." (Matthew 5:28–30).

6. **Do what you say you will do:** *"Let what you say be simply 'Yes' or 'No'; anything more than this comes from evil."* (Matthew 5:37).

7. **Love Your Enemies:** *"But I say to you, Love your enemies and pray for those who persecute you, so that you may be sons of your Father who is in heaven. For he makes his sun rise on the evil and on the good, and sends rain on the just and on the unjust. For if you love those who love you, what reward do you have? Do not even the tax collectors do the same?"* (Matthew 5:44–46).

8. **Invest in the kingdom:** *"Do not lay up for yourselves treasures on earth, where moth and rust destroy and where thieves break in and steal, but lay up for yourselves treasures in heaven, where neither moth nor rust destroys and where thieves do not break in and steal. For where your treasure is, there your heart will be also."* (Matthew 6:19–21).

9. **Seek God's Kingdom:** *"But seek first the kingdom of God and His righteousness, and all these things will be added to you."* (Matthew 6:33).

9. **Judge Not:** *"Judge not, that you be not judged. For with the judgment you pronounce you will be judged, and with the measure you use, it will be measured to you. Why do you see the speck that is in your brother's eye, but do not notice the log that is in your own eye?"* (Matthew 7:1–3).

10. **Pray for those that are called to preach full time:** *Then He said to His disciples, "The harvest is plentiful, but the laborers are few; therefore, pray earnestly to the Lord of the harvest to send out laborers into His harvest."* (Matthew 9:37–38).

11. **Fear Not:** *"And do not fear those who kill the body but cannot kill the soul. Rather fear him who can destroy both soul and body in hell."* (Matthew 10:28).

12. **Choose Christ's teachings and lifestyle:** *"Come to me, all who labor and are heavy laden, and I will give you rest. Take my yoke upon you, and learn from me, for I am gentle and lowly in heart, and you will find rest for your souls. For my yoke is easy, and my burden is light."* (Matthew 11:28–30).

13. **Forgive people who have wronged you:** *Then Peter came up and said to him, Lord, how often will my brother sin against me, and I forgive him? As many as seven times? Jesus said to him, "I do not say to you seven times, but seventy-seven times."* (Matthew 18:21–22).

14. **Honor your marriage:** *He answered, "Have you not read that He who created them from the beginning made them male and female, and said, Therefore, a man shall leave his father and his mother and hold fast to his wife, and the two shall become one flesh?"* (Matthew 19:4–6).

15. **Be willing to serve in even the smallest ways:** *"But whoever would be great among you must be your servant, and whoever would be first among you must be your slave, even as the Son of Man came not to be served but to serve, and to give His life as a ransom for many."* (Matthew 20:26–28).

16. **Be vigilant in waiting for Christ's return:** *"Therefore, stay awake, for you do not know on what day your Lord is coming. But know this, that if the master of the house had known in what part of the night the thief was coming, he would have stayed awake and would not have let his house be broken into. Therefore, you also*

must be ready, for the Son of Man is coming at an hour you do not expect." (Matthew 24:42–44).

17. **Participate in Holy Communion:** *Now as they were eating, Jesus took bread, and after blessing it broke it and gave it to the disciples, and said, "Take, eat; this is my body." And he took a cup, and when he had given thanks he gave it to them, saying, "Drink of it, all of you, for this is my blood of the covenant, which is poured out for many for the forgiveness of sins."* (Matthew 26:26–28).

18. **Share the Good News everywhere and all the time:** *"Go therefore and make disciples of all nations, baptizing them in the name of the Father and of the Son and of the Holy Spirit, teaching them to observe all that I have commanded you. And behold, I am with you always, to the end of the age."* (Matthew 28:19–20).

One of the things that separates us from grace is our unwillingness to follow all of Christ's commands. It is possible that it is our general willfulness. Possibly, we get lazy, and fall into bad habits which we have a difficult time breaking. Regardless, we are living in contradiction to Christ's instructions for us. Undoubtedly, Jesus identified the two commands that encompass all other instructions. Additionally, He also gave us instructions throughout His word about how these two commands should be lived.

In the rabbinical tradition, a teacher's point of view or take on the ancient texts was referred to as his yoke. Like a yoke that you would put on a pair of oxen, the image was to help students understand that once yoked to their teacher, they were to directly align themselves to him and his teachings. Jesus used this image when He said,

"Take my yoke upon you, and learn from me, for I am gentle and lowly in heart, and you will find rest for your souls. For my yoke is easy, and my burden is light."

Matthew 11:29-30 (ESV)

Making an "A" with God is neither possible nor desirable to try to attain. The teacher does not ask us to surpass Him or even be His equal! We are not in a class looking for a grade, but instead, we are on a journey walking with the Master and learning from His example.

<u>Chapter 3 Summary</u>

Key Points:

- We already have an "A" with the Father through Jesus, and on our own, regardless of our efforts, we will always score an "F".
- We are driven to succeed, even when success is already in our hands from God.
- Jesus has given us a broader set of commands in addition to commandments, and following these will lead to a deeper relationship with Him and a more thorough understanding of His nature.

Key Questions:

- What commands of Jesus do you find the hardest to accept?
- How does willfulness in your life separate you from receiving God's grace?
- Is there someone in your life that you need to show grace or unconditional love that you have been avoiding?

Prayer:

Lord, in the book of Matthew you wrote, "His lord said to him, 'Well done, good and faithful servant. You have been faithful over a little, I will set you over much. Enter into the joy of your master." We thank you for the commands and wisdom you have given us. We praise you for the thoroughness of your word in providing guidance for our lives. Please guide our every step to be to your glory and make us faithful over the generous gifts you have given us. We ask this in your Son's name. Amen.

Chapter 4: Nineveh Is in That Direction

"The heart of man plans his way, but the Lord establishes his steps."

Proverbs 16:9 ESV

One of my favorite stories in the Bible involves Jonah in the belly of the whale. It is not the whale, or the foreshadowing of Christ's death and resurrection that gets my attention. These are awesome components, but it is the bitterness of Jonah that is so intriguing to me. This is an angry guy that absolutely knew what God's will was and wanted nothing to do with it. Most of us pray to see God's will for us in our lives. It is no small irony that God was crystal clear about His will for Jonah, and Jonah was having none of it.

My prayers often contain the phrase, "Give me the courage to submit to your will, and then show your will to me." It used to be the other way around, but I figured out that I need the courage to submit first. Often, I suspect I know what God's will

41

for me is, but I don't have the courage to do what He is asking. My lack of courage comes from my interest in being the captain of my own ship, because I know what I am doing. Most of us believe we can do a pretty good job of running our own lives, thank you very much!

Unwillingness to submit to God is an impediment to accepting His grace.

Here is my summary of the story of Jonah, which has elements of courage, fear, rebellion and repentance throughout it. (Of course, for the full story, open your Bible to the book of Jonah):

Jonah gets a call from God . . . "Arise, go to Nineveh, that great city, and call out against it, for their evil has come up before me." (Jonah 1:2). Jonah hates Nineveh and doesn't like the demand of God for him to go try to save these rotten people. Jonah is smart enough to know that grumbling will not be sufficient to avoid this demand from God. So instead, Jonah becomes a man on the run and heads for the sea. How mad do you have to be at Nineveh to try to run away from God? Nineveh is East, and Jonah runs as far West as he can.

In a port town called Joppa, Jonah gets on a ship headed for Tarshish, a city that is a long way from Nineveh. His ship runs into a terrible storm that has clearly been created by the supernatural. God is with both this ship and Jonah, because He will not be ignored or denied. God is sovereign, and Jonah is not. The men on the ship do not know Jonah's God, and pray to their own gods trying to get the seas to calm. The seas do not calm.

Everyone fears that the ship will sink so they start looking for someone to blame, and their eyes settle on Jonah. When asked by his crew mates, "Who is your God?" Jonah says, "The God of heaven, who made the earth and the sea." Jonah is the cause of the storm, and he tells them that only throwing him in the sea will make it stop.

Now the sailors would prefer not to commit murder, so they try to row away from the storm. However, after trying to outrun God themselves, the sailors give up, throw Jonah overboard, and the sea is calm again. Meanwhile the trouble has just started for Jonah, who gets swallowed by a beast of the sea.

Three days in the fish hotel is a long time for Jonah. It is dark, awful, and it clearly gives a man some time to think. From the belly of the fish, Jonah cries out to God, and God has the fish hurl Jonah out on to the land. Does God punish Jonah, or chastise him, or explain Himself so that Jonah will come around to God's way of thinking? NO! God repeats His order exactly the way He had said it the first time, "Arise, go to Nineveh, that great city, and call out against it for their evil has come up before me." This time, Jonah starts walking.

Jonah does what God asks and preaches the need to repent throughout the city of Nineveh, and the message is heard by everyone all the way up to the king. The king takes a very practical approach to the message and says in Jonah 3:9, "Who knows? God may turn and relent and turn from His fierce anger, so that we may not perish." In Nineveh, the people hear his message and choose to repent. The city is spared, and this just does not sit well with Jonah.

Jonah hates Nineveh, and he basically tells God, 'See . . . this is why I did not want to tell them to repent, because I wanted them to die under your wrath. But see how You are . . . slow to anger and full of love? Oh, go ahead and kill me, because I cannot bear how bad this turned out for me, and I hate the fact that these people lived.' (In all fairness to the Word, above is my paraphrase).

In God's infinite patience, He does not smite Jonah (which is what God does, He is like the only one that gets to smite people). Now that Jonah has obeyed God, the Lord points out the error of Jonah's thinking and encourages him to see things from God's point of view.

Time out . . . isn't speaking with God supposed to be an amazing, positive and life changing event in a good way? How can Jonah turn his back on God? The God of heaven, who made the earth and the sea has spoken to a mere man. Do you think if you were Jonah you would have immediately headed for Nineveh?

Maybe Jonah is not a complete idiot, and actually has some reasons for not wanting to do what God asks right away. Why did Jonah hate Nineveh? Because Nineveh was the capital city of the one nation that continually made war and fought against the Jews, namely, Assyria. Eventually, it was Assyria that destroyed the Northern kingdom. To Jonah, going to Nineveh to preach to them so that they would repent and NOT be punished for what they did to the Jews was a terrible idea. Jonah wanted justice from God on Nineveh, not forgiveness. Jonah wanted revenge, not salvation.

Why did God want to save Nineveh? Because that is what God does, and who He is. This is part of the pattern of the Old Testament. God constantly tries to reconcile His people unto Himself. Time and again in the Old Testament, the people depart from God, His covenant and His instructions, only to suffer. Their suffering ultimately leads them back to God. This cycle has repeated itself from Adam to this very moment. Jonah sees a good for nothing city of 120,000 evildoers, and God sees a city of children that have lost their way. It is a matter of perspective.

> The Lord is not slow to fulfill his promise as some count slowness, but is patient toward you, not wishing that any should perish, but that all should reach repentance.
>
> **2 Peter 3:9 (ESV)**

Did God want just anyone to go speak to the people of Nineveh? No, God wanted Jonah to participate in saving these particular 120,000 people from destruction. Perhaps God really wanted to save 120,001? In the story, not only are the people of Nineveh saved, but so is Jonah. What message is God's Word sending us? He sends us several in this story:

1. Jonah was worth a lot of God's time and effort to save, and He used the redemption of Nineveh to teach Jonah about forgiveness, redemption and humility.
2. Nineveh was not beyond saving. God knew that if faced with the reality of their sin, they would repent. It is God's hope that the reality of our sin will cause us to repent too.
3. We all have a Nineveh in our lives that we need to walk to and through to share Christ's message of love and forgiveness.

So where is your Nineveh? Honestly, we all run from God's will from time to time. Where is God calling you to be reconciled, or preach His word, or reach out to someone in your life, or a group of someones in your life, that you are avoiding?

I have noticed in my own life that I spend a lot of time saving the saved. Nothing is more satisfying than spending time in worship, study or fellowship with my fellow Christians. As a matter of fact, I think I can safely say that everyone likes to reach out and spend time in fellowship with the faithful. Even in church, we spend time in meaningful conversations, building up each other in the faith. It is easy to save the saved, isn't it? But if I am honest, I don't go out of my way to share Jesus' love with non-believers. I don't have the courage to bring up the difference Jesus has made in my life with those that I don't know. Nineveh for me is the stranger that I meet every day and choose to avoid making "God contact" with.

You and I may be a great deal alike. Maybe for you, strangers are hard to evangelize to. Possibly the simple act of asking someone if you can pray for them, or the quoting of a Bible passage, seems too intrusive. Being labeled a 'Jesus freak,' or one of those church people, may be enough of a risk to keep you from talking about God to others. But just maybe, you also have a real-world Nineveh in your life that you are running from too.

Let's take a quick inventory and see if the Holy Spirit can help you identify the Nineveh in your life. I want you to imagine this scene . . .

You have been asked to give a talk and share your story, your path to faith, and what Jesus means to you. The Lord has put an important message into your heart, and you are going to share the things from inside that you have always avoided facing in public. God has put it on your heart that people in this room will be touched by the message He is sharing through you. But in the back of your mind, there is something holding you back. There is a face that you don't want to see in the room, there is someone that you are separated from, or someone you have never approached, because you don't want them to be close to you. There is someone that you don't want to hear your story, and you are scared to share your faith in Jesus with, because they might judge you. Can you see that person? Do you know their name? Is there more than one person?

Whomever you do not want to share Jesus with, that is where your Nineveh is. Will you have the courage to go there and share the Good News of Jesus? Will you tell that person about what Christ has meant to you in your life? Will you invite that person to experience God's love? Will you forgive that person for the pain they have caused you? Will you risk their judgment by sharing the truth about yourself? Will you risk further pain by being vulnerable? We are all Jonah, and we need to get busy preaching to our Nineveh.

We spend our lives looking for the right place to preach God's message. We pray for opportunities to share His love. We may even wander amongst strangers evangelizing as opportunities present themselves. Wouldn't it be fascinating if God had put all of our reaching and loving opportunities right in front of us in the people we want to touch the least? By breaking our own willfulness and being obedient, we will submit to God, and share Him even with those that we do not like or have not forgiven.

Chapter 4 Summary

Key Points:

- God is sovereign and when He asks, we do. It isn't easy, but it is simple.
- God does not have to explain Himself. After obedience, God may give you discernment, but obedience is first.
- It is easy to share our faith with believers, but we are called to share it with everyone.
- God instructs us to love those that we do not like, and this is a mission field for each of us.
- When you love those that hate you or do you wrong, God <u>may</u> soften their hearts, but He will certainly soften your heart.

Key Questions:

- What does it mean for God to be sovereign in your life?
- Do you suspect that you already know what God wants you to be doing for His kingdom?
- Can you think of a time that you knew God's will and followed it without question? How did that feel, and what happened?

- How clear does God's voice have to be for you to know that it is God?

- Where is your Nineveh? Where do you know that God wants you to share the message of salvation from His Son's death and resurrection? What is holding you back?

Prayer:

God, you are sovereign in my life, and I give my fear over to you. I want to share the love of Jesus with others. Thank you for the strangers you put in my path that I may share your love. Give me the courage to speak boldly about your Son and the salvation he purchased for all of us. God, I know that you have also placed a mission field in front of me in the people I know. Lord I ask you for the courage to share with people that have wronged me with the same passion and love I share with others. Your message is too powerful and too essential to pick and choose who receives it, so enable me to share it everywhere. I pray this in the name of Jesus Christ, my Lord and Savior. AMEN.

Chapter 5: Here Come the Pharisees

"Woe to you, scribes and Pharisees, hypocrites! For you are like whitewashed tombs, which outwardly appear beautiful, but within are full of dead people's bones and all uncleanness."

Matthew 23:27 (ESV)

You have to love the Pharisees in the Bible. For people that don't like lawyers, the Pharisees are a perfect foil for all things we don't like about supposedly educated people that stand on definitions and protocols to define our lives. Christ said that the Pharisees created, for others, rules and guidelines that they themselves could not live up to. Somewhere along the way during the Jewish captivity in Babylon, the religious leaders lost their way and started worrying more about the rules than the ruler. They got wrapped up in the things of this world instead of staying focused on the creator of all worlds. It is easy to see why. The Pharisees wanted a 'sure way' to please God, and if they followed 600+ rules to the letter, would that not be perfection? And by being perfect in their rule following, wouldn't that be pleasing to a perfect God? Remember an earlier chapter . . .they wanted an A even way back then!

Unfortunately, the process created a system of judgment and not a system of mercy. It created a system of exclusion, and not an opportunity to invite others to share in the treasure of God's love. Jesus said,

> "You hypocrites! Well did Isaiah prophesy of you, when he said: This people honors me with their lips, but their heart is far from me; in vain do they worship me, teaching as doctrines the commandments of men."
>
> **Matthew 15:7-9 (ESV)**

Yep, the Pharisees were alive and well 2,000 years ago, and they are still with us today, but we call them fellow Christians.

Denominationalism gets in the way of grace, and is just a fancy word for justifying our judgment of other Christians.

I wonder if people like the moral high ground because it gives them a better spot to look down on others from? In visiting many different Christian churches, it is clear that the message of Jesus Christ of love, grace and redemption is preached with vigor and enthusiasm. However, when the lights of the church are out, and believers meet in small groups or talk to others, the question of denomination and worship styles tends to creep into the conversation, and not in a good way. Why do Christians spend so much time judging each other and putting down each other's modest variations in belief and worship form? People think a lack of interest is what is destroying the Christian church, I think it is exactly the opposite, it is too much self-interest. We spend time discussing what form of worship will be most pleasing to God; whether guitars, projector screens, and female readers are appropriate in the liturgy, and a host of other form-based topics.

When I was a kid at St. Richard's grade school in Omaha, Nebraska, my fourth-grade teacher, Sister Mary Esther, (yes, this was really her name), equated Christianity to a multi-faceted diamond. On the black-board she drew a very large and improbably cut diamond with hundreds of facets. She proceeded to shade in certain amounts of the stone to illustrate how many of the true beliefs were shared with the Catholic faith by other denominations. Thankfully, I can still remember that Lutheran, my chosen expression of faith later in life, was the largest at around 90%. However, the nun in the traditional habit, with an ever-ready ruler for discipline, was careful to warn us that only a full diamond could make it into heaven. Although the others were good people, and trying hard, only the Catholics would enter into the Kingdom of Heaven because we were the only ones with the pure faith. It would be easy to say that this narrow thinking was restricted to Catholics, but that is not the case. Factions have crept into the Christian faith that express everything from a distaste for other denominations to outright denial of their access to the Kingdom of Heaven.

Even at ten years old, this picture of the right and wrong of denominations was weird to me. I had heard for so long that Jesus wanted us to "make disciples of all nations . . . and teach them everything I have commanded you." As an altar boy, I had often wondered what altar boys looked like in Jesus' time and what church must have been like. It struck me then as it does now that Jesus had a lot less ceremony and formality in His worship and prayer than we do. Jesus was the ultimate leader of an inclusive faith. He would not think of discarding even the most broken of gemstones from His Crown of Glory.

This divide and destroy system is not just for modern Christians. Old time Christians, Jews, Muslims, Hindus and every other major faith share the same internal struggles that we have. There is a human, and therefore sinful, need to always be 'one up' on someone else. Even in our faith and our churches, you will hear people compare preachers, music, length of service, and other elements of corporate worship on the scale of their own personal desire. In the Bible, this is a problem for the early Church, and Paul addresses the Church in Corinth in this way:

"I appeal to you, brothers, by the name of our Lord Jesus Christ, that all of you agree, and that there be no divisions among you, but that you be united in the same mind and the same judgment. For it has been reported to me by Chloe's people that there is quarreling among you, my brothers. What I mean is that each one of you says, 'I follow Paul,' or 'I follow Apollos,' or 'I follow Cephas,' or 'I follow Christ.' Is Christ divided? Was Paul crucified for you? Or were you baptized in the name of Paul? . . . . For Christ did not send me to baptize but to preach the gospel, and not with words

of eloquent wisdom, lest the cross of Christ be emptied of its

power. For the word of the cross is folly to those who are

perishing, but to us who are being saved it is the power of

God. "

1 Corinthians 1:10-13, 17-18 (ESV)

For the longest time, Jews believed that God lived in a box

behind a curtain in a building at the center of Jerusalem. The

Holy of Holies in the Temple was where the Ark of the Covenant

was kept, and God met the high priest once a year in that

location. In essence if you weren't on the Temple Mount, your

interaction with God was at best a hit and miss proposition, and

at worst, it was a waste of time. Jesus explained it this way to

the Samaritan woman . . .

"Woman," Jesus replied, "believe me, a time is coming when

you will worship the Father neither on this mountain nor in

Jerusalem. You Samaritans worship what you do not know;

we worship what we do know, for salvation is from the Jews.

Yet a time is coming and has now come when the true

worshipers will worship the Father in the Spirit and in truth,

for they are the kind of worshipers the Father seeks. God is spirit, and his worshipers must worship in the Spirit and in truth."

John 4:21-24 (NIV)

It comes down to the question of tent size. Does your faith have a big tent that has room for everyone that believes, or is it a pup tent that will only hold a few folks that worship exactly the same way that you do? Do you let the politics of interdenominational issues get in the way of your fellowship with other believers? I have a strange definition for politics. I think politics is the friction and damage created when we spend time measuring ourselves against each other, instead of measuring our progress toward a shared goal. Church politics is looking at each other for comparison instead of community. It gets in the way of the valuable focus which is created by everyone turning instead to the Cross.

Even on the night that Jesus was betrayed, the issue of pre-eminence amongst those that would lead Christ's mission on earth came up.

A dispute also arose among them, as to which of them was to be regarded as the greatest. And he said to them, "The kings of the Gentiles exercise lordship over them, and those in authority over them are called benefactors. But not so with you. Rather, let the greatest among you become as the youngest, and the leader as one who serves. For who is the greater, one who reclines at table or one who serves? Is it not the one who reclines at table? But I am among you as the one who serves."

Luke 22:24-27 (ESV)

If it happened amongst those people physically closest to and chosen by Jesus, of course it would happen to us.

Jesus wanted life as a believer to be uncomplicated. He recognized that the Pharisees and Sadducees had encumbered His Father's guidance to a point where a perpetual failure was all that was possible. His instructions to His followers were to be simple and goal oriented. The question should be, "Once you are saved, what are Christ's expectations, not for salvation, but for living the life of a Child of God in community with other believers?"

"Be completely humble and gentle; be patient, bearing with one another in love. Make every effort to keep the unity of the Spirit through the bond of peace. There is one body and one Spirit, just as you were called to one hope when you were called; one Lord, one faith, one baptism; one God and Father of all, who is over all and through all and in all."

Ephesians 4:2-6 (NIV)

Means of worship and praise are not narrowly defined by God in a liturgical sense. Being a Pharisee is like being a sinner . . . it is the state that we all start in. We all start by trying to earn our way to heaven through works and actions. We all want a blueprint that is complicated and hard, but that through our own efforts, will lead us to a better outcome. Jesus forgives us our willfulness and our attitudes about this. He smiles and says to us, "Don't work so hard at this, and don't put so many burdens upon yourselves." Jesus gives the comfort of our real role, and that is of student and friend.

"Come to me, all who labor and are heavy laden, and I will give you rest."

Matthew 11:28 (ESV)

<u>Chapter 5 Summary</u>

Key Points:

- Comparative denominationalism is a very human, and therefore very sinful, behavior that separates believers. The measuring stick of a person's "Christianity" is held by God and not by us.

- God's definition of liturgy and church worship is more about sincerity and persistence than structure.

- Method of worship does not earn salvation. For the saved, worship is not a requirement, but a heartfelt desire to express our love and gratitude to the Triune God.

Key Questions:

- Why was Jesus so angry at the Pharisees, and how do we act in the same way today?

- What challenges regarding denominationalism keep you from embracing fellow Christians?

- How can you bring others to know Christ without imposing structure or tradition as a requirement for acceptance into His family?

Prayer:

God, you sent your only Son to live and pay the price for all sins, past, present and future, for all people. Thank you for the gift of salvation and the opportunity to be called your child. Help me to remember that everyone I meet is my brother or sister and that they are no more or less saved than me. Help me to lead the lost, the unreached and the unrepentant with the love you have shown me. I pray this in the name of Jesus Christ, my Lord and Savior. AMEN.

Chapter 6: God Gave Us Free Will, and He Wants It Back

"I call heaven and earth to witness against you today, that I have set before you life and death, blessing and curse. Therefore choose life, that you and your offspring may live, loving the Lord your God, obeying his voice and holding fast to him, for he is your life and length of days, "

Deuteronomy 30:19-20 (ESV)

What has free will ever done for you? Seriously! My free will has led me into poor decisions, addiction, pain, suffering, and yet, I will claw and fight if someone tries to take it away from me. I want to make my own decisions, and not be controlled by anyone or anything. It is that need for freedom which exerts the greatest dominance over my life. My need for freedom actually drives out common sense, good intentions, a life of training, a relationship with God, and on and on. It is amazing how much the freedom of free will ultimately robs me of control.

Conversations about free will often devolve into discussions about choice. It is interesting because God did not give us unlimited choice or unlimited will. He gave us the ability to choose His will or our will. It is not a large number of choices, it is actually only one choice that is measured out innumerably every day in the way we live our lives.

Demanding our own will stands in the way of the full measure of grace we are to receive.

When we pray the Lord's prayer, we say, "thy will be done on earth as it is in heaven." However, I think I really would prefer that it read, "my will be done on earth and your will be done in heaven, unless your will and my will happen to be the same on a specific issue." If we are honest, our hope is that God's will and our own will are the same, and therefore we get a double win.

God's message to us is simple . . . Choose my will! When the people of Israel would choose to be willful and to pursue other gods and ignore God's commands, He would punish them like a very angry disciplinarian father and attempt to bring them back to His will. The Old Testament has dozens of examples of this cycle of willfulness, suffering at the hands of godless nations, prophetic reminders of God's will, repentance, reconciliation and freedom. The rod of punishment was used to bring His people back to Him. They hated to submit to His will, but they ultimately hated the consequences of their own choice to abandon Him even more. I have a lot in common with the Israelites!

Choosing to live according to your own will has consequences. These consequences are designed to help us understand that although we have the choice, we should choose wisely. When we fail to choose wisely, God will use these consequences to guide us back to Him. Make no mistake, God does not create the consequences, because He does not have to. The outcomes from our sinful choices are going to be painful.

"When tempted, no one should say, "God is tempting me." For God cannot be tempted by evil, nor does he tempt anyone; but each person is tempted when they are dragged away by their own evil desire and enticed. Then, after desire has conceived, it gives birth to sin; and sin, when it is full-grown, gives birth to death."

James 1:13-15 (NIV)

Living according to our own will always leads to sin. Whether right away or over time, sin in all ways leads to pain. Pain always drives us to further sin, and fear. This cycle is the outcome of our decision to try to do it our own way.

In this battle of wills, (His will vs. self-will), the only appropriate response is to surrender. No person in the Bible has ever struggled against the will of God and won. It is an impossibility! Being vulnerable is the first step on the road to surrender. Life may beat us down. Our own choices may cause us to suffer. However, it is when like the Israelites, we cry out to God for mercy and grace that we can feel His redemptive love as we submit to His will. God knows the pattern only too well. Our will weakens our relationship toward God, but never weakens His relationship toward us. Our turning from Him causes damage sufficient to turn us back to Him.

I try to turn my will over to God because frankly, He is infinitely more qualified to run my life than I am. Every day is like driver's education class. There are two steering wheels in the car of my life, and I am constantly trying to wrest control from the other driver. I know very well that the expert driver is sitting in the driver's seat, and I am in the seat on the right, but for some reason instead of enjoying the ride, I keep trying to stop the car, speed it up, or cause an accident by swerving in one direction or another. Time and again, the consequences of my actions remind me that I am not a very good driver of the car of my life.

God's will for you in the world.

Many of us feel that God has called us for a special ministry in the world. It may be a soup kitchen, or helping people learn to read, or sharing the love of God in a foreign land. Regardless, many of us picture a ministry in which we play a key if not pivotal role in the ministry's success for the glory of God. We are just not sure which ministry it is, so we wait for a divine calling to point us in the right direction. Unfortunately, the work of the kingdom which would benefit from our help languishes while we wait.

"Then he said to his disciples, "The harvest is plentiful, but the laborers are few; therefore pray earnestly to the Lord of the harvest to send out laborers into his harvest."

Matthew 9:37-38 (ESV)

I wonder if the laborers Christ is referencing are us, just waiting on the sidelines, hoping to receive a sign that it is time to get into the field. Well intentioned and willing, we delay engaging for fear that working fervently in one area of ministry will cause us to somehow miss our true calling. What if it all is our true calling?

Jesus was indiscriminate in His ministry. He fed thousands, He healed people, He preached the Good News, He trained future leaders, He helped widows, and He did it all the time. His ministry was simply described by Him when he said, "I do what I have seen the Father do." He did not wait for a unique calling, His life was His unique calling, and so is yours!

In pursuit of His will, I have often prayed, "Lord, show me your will and give me the courage to submit to it." I liked this prayer, and being sinful, I was actually proud of this prayer. I would pray it aloud, and I would add it to the end of prayers said in groups. To my thinking, the submission to God's will would take great courage, and identifying His will would require substantial effort. Sometimes, I just have to laugh at myself. What a classic misunderstanding goofball I am!

Some key concepts that have repeatedly expressed themselves in my life are:

1. God's will is not trying to express itself in my life. His will is always expressing itself, and my life is part of His will.

2. God does not have a plan for my life, He has a plan. My life is part of that plan, but His plan will be fulfilled whether or not I join Him with my feeble efforts.

3. God loves me completely. He wants me to align and be an active part of His plan and has work He wants me to do. However, He is not going to wait for me to be inspired or 'discover' my calling to move His plan along.

4. It is not God's will for me to have a unique and special ministry to bring glory to Him, and I just have to figure out what that ministry is. Rather, ministry opportunities are presented to me every day, and I should join each of them as I am called. If I am to lead, He will ask me to lead, and if I am to follow, He will let me follow. He is doing the doing, and I am His hands and feet.

I still pray the same prayer, but my emphasis is now more on my submission than anything else!

God's will is that we be satisfied with Him.

At this point, it would be easy to think that you as an individual, are not special to God. Possibly to contemplate that no unique place in the universe is set aside for you to make a difference for Him. This is very far from the truth. God's will for the world and his will for you are the same. He wants everyone to know Him personally and feel His love and grace through His son, Jesus Christ. He wants everyone to have the Holy Spirit dwell within them and to be shared with others so that we can all be one, as the Trinity is one. He also wants us to understand the generosity of this opportunity, and to recognize it as more than sufficient.

You might say to yourself, "I just know that God wants me to make a big difference for His Kingdom. I am on fire for Jesus and I am sure that He has something special He wants me to do." His definition of "making a big difference," and what is "special" is entirely different than ours.

"For my thoughts are not your thoughts,
   neither are your ways my ways, declares the Lord.
For as the heavens are higher than the earth,

so are my ways higher than your ways

and my thoughts than your thoughts."

Isaiah 55:8-9 (ESV)

Remember, His real hope for us is to be one with Him. Jesus said it to us in the book of John,

"That they may all be one, just as you, Father, are in me, and I in you, that they also may be in us, so that the world may believe that you have sent me. The glory that you have given me I have given to them, that they may be one even as we are one, I in them and you in me, that they may become perfectly one, so that the world may know that you sent me and loved them even as you loved me."

John 17:21-23 (ESV)

Being one with the Father starts with being one with our fellow Christians. He looks down from heaven, and asks, "Why do you have to make this so much harder than it has to be?" God's will for us in part is to **live, love and share.** That may seem pretty straightforward and almost pithy. However, His will leaves a lot of the day-to-day work in the living, loving and sharing up to us.

Live

The concept of living rarely goes mentioned these days without the concept of quality of life accompanying the thought. For this reason, it is typical to think of our lives on earth as requiring better things, better food, and better shelter as a means to demonstrate that God is taking care of us in the way that we deserve as His children. This is a false teaching, but from the very beginning, the concept of a faith that brings prosperity has been used to tempt the faithful. Although prosperity evangelism has been made popular by television-based ministers, I think they misinterpret what God promises in terms of how we are going to live on earth. God promises us "our daily bread," and that He will provide whatever we truly need. No one can possibly think that they know more about what we really need than God.

Our wanting comes from a fear that only more will make us feel better. The problem with more is that it is as a concept intrinsically tied to "never enough." Once you become a slave to the master of more, you can never be content because the hole in your need can never be filled. Paul tells us that he has learned how to be content in all things.

"I have learned in whatever situation I am to be content. I know how to be brought low, and I know how to abound. In any and every circumstance, I have learned the secret of facing plenty and hunger, abundance and need. I can do all things through him who strengthens me."

Philippians 4:11-13 (ESV)

This oneness that God desires manifests itself in a sense of peace and contentment. When Paul says, "I can do all things through him who strengthens me," his reference is to being at one with the Father and His will for what is sufficient and necessary. God is enough!

Love

One of the most quoted scriptures in the Bible relates to the two great commandments.

"You shall **love** the Lord **your God with all your heart** and with **all your** soul and with **all your** mind. ... And a second is like it: You shall **love your** neighbor as yourself. On these two commandments depend all the Law and the Prophets."

Matthew 22:37-40 (ESV)

This concept was new to me when I got my head wrapped around the transitional phrase, "And a second is like it". We are to love Him first **and in the same way** He loves us, we are to love others. God gives us two instructions instead of one to avoid the inevitable loophole we would create about not having to love other people. If God wanted us to worry only about Him, He would have told us! He wants us to be focused on the rest of His creation as well.

Additionally, He wants our love to be like the way we love Him . . . completely engaged with our hearts, souls and minds. For God, there are not two kinds of love. There is one approach to love which it total and consuming. However, although the love is to be the same that comes from us, there are two priorities.

We must first love God completely. Why Him first? It seems that if God lives in each of us, the shortcut would be to just love people. Many existentialists and atheists believe that loving their fellow man is really all that is necessary to be a good person. They point to the benefits of other centeredness, of doing good, and of a life built around works as noble and fulfilling. But Jesus' point to us in Matthew is that we will never be able to truly understand the type of unconditional love and relationship we are supposed to have with others until we first seek to experience it with the Father. The order is important, because for us to get good at what real love is towards others, we must first understand it from the source of that love . . . God!

Share

Sharing is not easy. Try to take even the smallest toy from a child, and you will see the future adult pull violently and exclaim, "MINE!" It is because we are fearful of losing things that Christ wants us to share. For years I have heard the pastors exhort me to "give to the Lord what is His." I am a person that tithes, and I believe whole-heartedly in tithing. As much as I have heard about tithing, I don't hear a lot about sharing. Tithing and sharing are not the same thing. The tithe is an acknowledgement that all things are God's, and that a portion of what He has given us needs to be cheerfully returned in order to conduct the mission of the church. Sharing is about recognizing need as we see it, and then seizing the opportunity to be Jesus in the world.

Here are several passages from Jesus about sharing that give us a clear picture of what we are to do with what we are given, after we have provided for the needs of the church.

- And He answered them, "Whoever has two tunics is to share with him who has none, and whoever has food is to do likewise." **Luke 3:11**
- And Jesus, looking at him, loved him, and said to him, "You lack one thing: go, sell all that you have and give to the poor, and you will have treasure in heaven; and come, follow me." Disheartened by the saying, he went away sorrowful, for he had great possessions. **Mark 10:21**
- Sell your possessions and give to the needy. Provide yourselves with moneybags that do not grow old, with a treasure in the heavens that does not fail, where no thief approaches and no moth destroys. For where your treasure is, there will your heart be also. **Luke 12:33-34**
- For I was hungry, and you gave me food, I was thirsty and you gave me drink, I was a stranger and you welcomed me, I was naked and you clothed me, I was sick and you visited me, I was in prison and you came to me.' **Matthew 25:35-36**

- Give, and it will be given to you. Good measure, pressed down, shaken together, running over, will be put into your lap. For with the measure you use it will be measured back to you." **Luke 6:38**

Living, loving and sharing are God's will for our lives. When we live in that will, the path is not always easy, but is not as perilous. Jesus told us that we are to be yoked to Him. We are to live a life that is as much like His as it can be, and the rewards will be both on this earth and through eternity.

<u>Chapter 6 Summary</u>

Key Points:

- The only choice truly presented to us by God when He gave us free will, is to choose His will or our own. All other choices proceed from this first choice.

- God's will for us to minister does not wait for us to sense a special calling. Rather, his will is being worked out around us all the time. It is our responsibility to align our lives to that will by working in ministry for the benefit of His kingdom.

- Being at one with God, as Jesus is within the Trinity is the ultimate expression of surrender to God's will. This oneness removes the impediments to grace of dissatisfaction and envy by allowing us to be content in the gifts that He has provided.

Key Questions:

- If you took an inventory of your life, where would you say that you are aligned to God's will in this world, and where have you chosen to let your will govern?

- Where is God's will to help others, to minister, to share the word of Christ happening around you today, and how can you join those efforts?
- In each of the key areas of living, loving and sharing, how can a change in the way you are thinking result in a change in the way you live?

Prayer:

Lord, your will is ever present and always evident in my life. Thank you for not hiding your will from me, but constantly casting a bright light upon it so that I can see. I often lack the courage on my own to choose your will due to the irrational fears I try to face alone. Please give me your strength to face my fears and work along others inside your will. I ask this in the name of Jesus, who chose your will when it mattered most. Amen.

Chapter 7: Fishers of Men Have to Have Bait

"While walking by the Sea of Galilee, He saw two brothers, Simon (who is called Peter) and Andrew his brother, casting a net into the sea, for they were fishermen. And He said to them, "Follow me, and I will make you fishers of men." Immediately they left their nets and followed him. And going on from there He saw two other brothers, James the son of Zebedee and John his brother, in the boat with Zebedee their father, mending their nets, and He called them. Immediately they left the boat and their father and followed him."

Matthew 4:18-22 (ESV)

My friend Gary used to tell stories about fishing in Nebraska and Colorado. He would tie flies, and go to fishing shops, and talk to folks about what was the right lure to use for the fish in that area. If he found someone particularly knowledgeable, he would ask things like, "Would you put a pork rind on the end of that Johnson silver spoon?" Such was the language of the avid fisherman. It made no sense to me, but those that knew their business, would nod sagely or offer an equally impossible to decipher alternative.

Christ told the disciples as he tells us, "Follow me, and I will make you fishers of men." What did He mean? What kinds of people will we be fishing for, and what kind of bait should we use? Of course, all analogies fall apart at some point, but if we are going to be fishing for men, we should examine the types of individuals we will run across and think about what kinds of conversations we might have, as well as what kind of bait we should use. Any good fisherman knows, it is not just the setting of the hook that takes skill, it is the managing of the catch to the boat which requires the most effort.

At this point, you might wonder, "Has he lost his mind? Does he honestly believe our evangelical role is to trick people to bite at a hook of false hope, (which is what bait is to a fish), only to reel them in?" Not at all, but I believe that when Jesus told his disciples that He would make them "fishers of men," He was not just speaking in a metaphor or euphemistically. He wanted them, and us, to bring the catch home to Him and to use all means possible to win people to Christ. Paul said,

"To the weak I became weak, that I might win the weak. I have become all things to all people, that by all means I might save some."

1 Corinthians 9:22 (ESV)

Sharing grace and faith are a requirement for a Christian, and not an option.

Paul was not a fisherman by trade, but through Christ, he developed the skills necessary to be a fisher of men, a planter of churches, and a disrupter of mistaken tradition.

When the Inuit Indians, (often called Eskimos), went out to hunt a whale, everyone on the boat had a specific role. The harpooner took care of the tackle and was responsible for harpooning the whale, the oarsmen rowed, the shaman sang to the whales, and so on. Peter, James, and John, also went fishing as a group and gathered their fish in nets, but with each member of the team having a role. When we share the word of God and seek to bring people to Christ, we must remember, we are not alone. We have the Holy Spirit as our partner in this fishing expedition. We must remember that we are capable of bringing someone to know of Christ, but only the Holy Spirit can lead someone to a relationship with Christ.

We must avoid the temptation to land a big fish with a single cast, and club it into submission on the deck of the boat, like we were going after a Marlin off the coast of Florida. God is not seeking someone that has been bludgeoned, or through guilt, forced to make a half-hearted and reluctant declaration of faith. That would be human and an inadequate beginning to a real relationship. God wants an open and tender heart that has seen through the masquerade of self -pride and human failings and seeks communion with the Creator.

As fishermen, we are to cast the "bread of life" upon the waters and share our faith from a place of personal conviction. The bread of life is Jesus. Jesus can take many forms in our efforts to share. He can be testimony, a life of Christian example, prayers offered and responded to, the word of God in the Bible, and even more. When we cast the bread upon the waters, a variety of different types of people may rise to the bait. However, for every fish, the bait should differ if you want to become an expert at the craft. What kinds of fish are there in the lake of men?

The Waiters

I love Westerns, and without a doubt, John Wayne was the master of that genre. I think it was his certainty and confidence that gave him such a presence on the screen. His characters never questioned themselves, and rarely worried about their own actions. It seemed like John Wayne's characters just knew what it meant to be a man in the Old West. He had the confidence and swagger of a leader.

With all that on-screen certainty, what was John Wayne's off-screen faith like? His family reports that John Wayne was a deathbed convert. Although he had tinkered with spirituality and faith his entire life, it was in the closing reel of the movie of his life that he let the Holy Spirit enter his heart for real.

There are stories of those that waited until they were at the door to eternity to hear the voice of Jesus and to accept Him into their hearts. Are the people that wait and wonder truly saved? Of course, they are:

"because, if you confess with your mouth that Jesus is Lord and believe in your heart that God raised him from the dead, you will be saved. For with the heart one believes and is justified, and with the mouth one confesses and is saved."

Romans 10:9-10 (ESV)

Why do they wait until the last second? A better question might be why anyone waits at all! Is it our failure as evangelists to truly point out the joy we find in Jesus? Is it a messaging problem that Christians face? Maybe people believe that when you truly give your life to Christ and live a life of acknowledged grace, you also live a life of stark boredom! A Christian life is not one of scarcity in pleasure, but one of true abundance of joy. Few of us started our adult lives with a full acceptance of Christ not just as Savior, but also as Lord. For that reason, we need to meet people where we find them in their journey. Their path will have been different than ours, their attitudes and beliefs will be different, and their acceptance of their condition of sin and need for redemption will also be different from our own.

The Seekers that are Hopeful

Among all the categories that sociologists can use for the religious status of people, the most under reported may be the seekers. These people are classified by words like seeker, agnostic or deist, but for the most part a better term could be considered *hopeful*. It is not a lack of interest which keeps them from the altar, it is a lack of trust. "Is it real? No, I mean is it really real?" This is the question of the seeker. When we peel back all the thinking and doubts, they want to know what we all want to know . . . "Is Christ real, and can He be real for me?" All other questions hinge on this one fundamental query.

As a salesman myself, I have always thought that a sales pitch is wasted on someone who already wants to buy. If a buyer wants to buy, who am I to get in their way with a lot of useless words? Often this means a person has been shopping and has already made the decision to buy. In essence, they don't need to have faith in my words as a salesperson because they have researched the facts for themselves. If this is true for someone I meet, the need for faith has been replaced by fact and I am simply a vessel to help transact the sale.

For seekers, it is a connection between the God you know and the God they want to know that is absent. Our role is to connect or be a bridge from their interest to their action. Seekers hunger for spiritual food and want to see what the promise of a relationship will deliver. In short, they want to meet Jesus, and they are hoping that they can find someone that can lead the way. More importantly, they would truly love to meet someone that has become the way by becoming like Jesus. For the seeker, we need to share the Jesus we know through our actions, our devotion, our prayer, our words, our worship and our lives. Then we need to ask them to join us in each of those activities, one at a time.

The Uninformed and the Uninterested

Many books refer to the Latin origins of the word religion and rightly recognize the word's meaning as, "to bind". Self-righteous folks, (like myself), may even say that religion tends to not only bind, but ensnare its practitioners. People have a great deal of judgment about churches that they have never been in, believers they have never met, and a Bible they have never read. Often, they have prejudged faith and religion based upon a skewed or incomplete understanding of what these things are.

Religious prejudice is as prevalent as racial or economic prejudice, and it is equally misguided and dangerous.

I have often heard that knowledge is the death of learning. This makes sense, and we all know someone that "you can't tell anything to because they already think they know everything!" Educating someone that is full of themselves and their own opinions is like doing magic before cows. How do you break through? YOU DON'T. In all experiences in which the desire is to introduce Jesus Christ, you are not doing the doing! For that reason, the notion of storming the well-guarded castle of a person's resolve will be fruitless. The Holy Spirit must do the doing, but we can still do God's work in addition to praying.

It is easier to enter the castle through the front gate than to assail the ramparts. For someone that believes they know many things, nothing is more enticing than someone that will listen to them. Through your questions and active listening, a knowing person can sometimes discover something that they don't know. The key to an exchange of this nature is to avoid the temptation to make an argument. The dialog is simply a means to unlock the person's thought process and allow them to examine things in detail. The combination of prayer and compassionate listening will do more to create an open heart and mind than all the arguments you can muster. Listen, listen some more, and when it feels like you should say something, go ahead and ask a question.

The Former and the Opposed

The most adamant opponents to Jesus Christ and organized religion are often former believers and members of the Body. We all run across former believers that have fallen away from the faith. Sometimes, their adamant denial of what they once held as truth in a way becomes their new faith. They are passionate in their disbelief. They wear their frustration and disappointment in God as a badge of honor or a scarlet letter of scorn.

Those that are opposed to faith, are oftentimes individuals that espouse spiritual connectedness, but want to be unconnected to religion. Different denominations or Christianity in general have let them down. They have experienced hypocrisy and judgment and lacked a sense of belonging in their journey. Rather than feel segregated in someone else's church, they separate themselves from everyone else.

The former believers and fanatical opponents to faith desperately want to believe. Their passion is an indication of the level of pain and distrust that they feel. Their experience is probably not unique, but it feels unique to them, and they want someone to listen to their fear, doubt and anger before providing them the hope of a previously abandoned solution. The process of listening may take a very long time.

The Blue Light Special

The faith shoppers, and those that pick from the buffet of belief systems, are still really just seekers in disguise. This pick and choose approach to faith asserts that a human being can discern which elements of each of the world view systems is the most appropriate to their own life. What that really means is most appropriate to their own lifestyle. By selection of methods of salvation, or rituals of alignment to the cosmos, people put themselves at the very center of their universe. When you choose to make it up from whole cloth or everyone else's belief set, how can you ever be judged or be sinful? The rules are made up by you, and therefore, you are always right!

What is the nature of Christian faith and the receipt of the message? Christ told a wonderful parable of the nature of faith and belief in the form of scattered seed:

"Listen! A farmer went out to plant some seeds. As he scattered them across his field, some seeds fell on a footpath, and the birds came and ate them. Other seeds fell on shallow soil with underlying rock. The seeds sprouted quickly because the soil was shallow. But the plants soon wilted under the hot sun, and since they didn't have deep roots, they died. Other seeds fell among thorns that grew up and choked out the tender plants. Still other seeds fell on fertile soil, and they produced a crop that was thirty, sixty, and even a hundred times as much as had been planted! Anyone with ears to hear should listen and understand."

Matthew 13: 3-9 (NLT)

When we come across those believers for whom the fire has dwindled, or the faith has diminished in importance, what should we do? Do we chastise them for their flagging energy, or possibly beg them to return with us to a love relationship with Jesus that might heal them of their apathy, frustration or challenges? I believe, that like the seeds that were planted in the parable, we need to first look at the soil. What is the spiritual condition of the person we are talking to? Where in their life are we finding them? Has something happened that has created this malaise or active disinterest, or has nothing happened at all, and that is the real issue?

Without understanding the soil, simply applying more seed will inevitably lead to another undesirable outcome. We need to listen first, second, and third; and then love them back to Christ. It may not be easy, and there may be real wounds that require cleansing and addressing, but in the end, only fertile soil will yield a harvest for Jesus.

Jesus promised His disciples to make them fishers of men. He gave us the great commission, and we are to go out and in essence become fishers of men as well. So . . . what bait are you using?

1. *Words.* I talk a lot. Sometimes I listen, I think, but I KNOW that I talk a lot! In my words, I have trained myself to weave the story of God's blessings in my life; not because I deserve them, but because He has chosen to bless me, and I am grateful. When asked, "How are you today?", my response is invariably, "Blessed and Highly Challenged!" This brings a smile to most people's faces, and they reference the blessed part or they comment on the challenged part. What they don't do, is ignore this interesting turn of a phrase. The phrase begs a response from a truly interested listener. It baits them to ask questions, and to seek more through fellowship, albeit brief, with me.

2. *Life of Christian Action.* St. Francis of Assisi is widely quoted as saying, "Preach the gospel, and if necessary, use words." If we live a life of Christian action, preaching is not necessary. The more like Christ we become, the less judging, and the more truly loving we will be. In this condition and by living a life that is emblematic in this way, people will be drawn to you. They will ask, "Why are you joy filled, loving and decent?" and then they will ask, "How can I be more like you?"

3. *Prayer.* Public prayer is not easy for most people. When

people from my congregation are asked to pray with each other over someone, or to pray about something in a small group, it is often uncomfortable for many. However, prayer, and the promise of prayer on someone's behalf, can be uplifting to them and to you. When someone tells me about an illness, upcoming surgery or difficulty in their life or the life of someone close to them, I say like many of us, "Well, I will include them in my prayers."

Recently however, I have said the same thing, and then I have asked permission to pray with the person in front of me right then, regardless of where we are. It is not a long prayer, but by joining in prayer, I know that Jesus is present as He promised. In this way, the commitment of prayer is made and realized simultaneously, and I have shown the person I am with that Jesus is real to me and that prayer is not just something I say to imply interest.

Secondly, I make a note of the prayer that we have shared, and I follow up later. I am desperately interested in watching God at work in people's lives. He is amazing and wonderful, and in addition to my prayers for them, I want to celebrate in prayerful thanksgiving what God does for them. The petition can be easy, but we all forget to say thank you, and a prayer of gratitude needs to be delivered as well.

Sometimes prayers are answered very differently than we hope. A bad diagnosis, a relapse in treatment, or a failed pregnancy are all moments of tremendous sadness. It is even more important at those times that I have been available to provide prayers of certainty in God's will, and sometimes anger at our inability to understand Him.

4. *Physical.* I am not very fashion conscious. My brother says that my personal brand statement is "Comfortable". Therefore, unless otherwise required, I spend my days in jeans, shorts, t-shirts and sweatshirts. However, as Jeff Foxworthy has pointed out, you can tell a lot about a man's vacations, hobbies and favorite things by the messages on his clothes. For some, it is about beer, cigarettes, Nascar, football/basketball/baseball or fishing, but for me it is often about Jesus. I just can't resist a good-looking t-shirt that has a compelling faith-based message.

Additionally, I picked up a rubber bracelet several years ago that was multicolored and had the key words of faith all around it. Words inscribed included Faith, Forgiveness, Grow, Heaven,

Sin and Blood. This bracelet is a little out of the norm, and it gets a fair number of comments. When people ask me about it, I take off the bracelet and hand it to them, and then pull a card that comes along with the item out of my wallet to share with them. This is a short testimony card that I ask them to keep along with the bracelet. Our exchange may take three minutes, but I have been able to plant the seed into the ground that the Holy Spirit placed in front of me. Of course, I have dozens of these at home to share as the moments arise, and I simply put on another, put a card in my wallet, and wait for the soil that He has made ready.

The purpose of using these tools is to draw people in and let them know that Jesus is accessible . . .and so are you! You are merely declaring your love for Him, and your willingness to share that love in the form of conversation, testimony, a listening ear, a non-judgmental shoulder to cry on, a meal that can be shared, etc.

I am surprised how often someone will look at a Christian bracelet I am wearing, or respond to my comment, "Blessed and Highly Challenged," asking what that is all about. Similarly, when I pray over meals with clients, coworkers or simply with family in public, it often begins a dialog with them or strangers about Jesus. It may start with what church our family goes to, but it always moves to Him and how He touches our lives. We have cast the bread upon the waters, and the Holy Spirit has returned a bountiful harvest in the net.

<u>Chapter 7 Summary</u>

Key Points:

- We are all evangelists, and the question is what message does our life share?
- We must be prepared to plant the seed of God's love in whatever soil he presents to us.
- Sometimes the soil of opportunity is not ready to receive the seed, and we are also called to cultivate the soil as part of the sharing process.

Key Questions:

- What bait are you using to engage people in conversation with you about Jesus?
- Are there people in your life that fit one of the seeking categories above that you can reach out to for the purpose of cultivation?
- Are there parts of your own life that look like barren or weedy patches of soil that you need to ask God to cultivate and pour seed into?

Prayer:

Father, we want to be great fishermen and farmers for the harvest and yield that you have planted and created. Sometimes we tire in our efforts or are not sure what the right approach is. We ask you to guide our words and efforts, that they are of you and not of us, so that the outcome is always assured. Give us the courage to speak boldly and proclaim our faith honestly, everywhere we go. In your Son's name. Amen.

Chapter 8: On My Knees

"For the wages of sin is death, but the free gift of God is eternal life in Christ Jesus our Lord."

Romans 6:22 (ESV)

Through the scripture we learn that God will never give you more than you can handle. My belief is that God will never give you more than you can handle <u>with</u> Him, but He will always allow more than you can handle by yourself to crop up in your life. That's right, the pain, stress and issues in your life that pile up to what appears to be an insurmountable mountain, are there for a reason. The reason is that we live in a broken world, and not a world that God wanted for us. Additionally, the reason is to remind us that we are to rely on God. If we could do it all ourselves, we would not need God. By allowing the troubles of this sinful world to break us and bring us to our knees, God gives us the perfect reason for Himself . . . because we need Him!

Please understand, I am not saying that God is the cause of our troubles. No, God allows the troubles of this world to exist in our lives without simply removing them, but He does not create them. The world has enough trouble of its own by its very nature, that God does not have to create challenges to prove a point or increase our dependency upon Him. But as in all things that God uses to work out His will, these difficulties serve a purpose, and that purpose is to bring us back to Him.

Nobody comes to the father on their feet, we all come on our knees. We come by way of the cross. We're on our knees because life has put us there. The Lord allows that because it is good for us.

Unwillingness to kneel before the cross gets in the way of receiving grace.

When I was diagnosed with Stage IV lung cancer, it was overwhelming. That is to say, it was so surreal that I did not even know how to respond. It felt like it must be happening to someone else. My family and I talked regularly in the first few days about how this just did not seem like something that we were going to face, because . . .

- I have never been a smoker.
- I am in reasonably good shape (round is a shape!)
- I am too young (only just turning 52 at the time.)
- God has me engaged in too many things for His glory to take me out of the picture.
- We have too many plans for our future that should be pleasing to Him, and that we had worked too hard to create.

Without a doubt, I was coming to the cross on my feet. In many ways my excuses were my effort to look Jesus in the eye as He hung on the cross . . . as though we were equals. All the I, me, and my attitudes and thoughts were stumbling blocks that did not cause me to fall to my knees, but rather to keep trying to catch myself so He could see me and my self-righteousness. Clearly, I was worthy to spare!

You

Even my approach to the disease was fraught with ego and arrogance. I wrapped myself in my Bible, put on my hat of faith, assembled my army of prayer warriors and tried to assail the King with a petition for a miracle for "deserving me." My family and I came up with a theme verse for our Battle, (James 1:12), and our Battle Hymn became, *I Rise,* by Chris Tomlin. We bought bracelets that had the words, "Just Breathe" inscribed in them, and collected verses that were meaningful to us to use in reflection during the upcoming times of challenge. In short, we put on the Armor of God and rode out on our noble steeds to go to war with . . . with who?

And therein lies the rub. We were trying to manage our condition with ourselves PLUS God. We had not started with God, and added ourselves to His plan, but started with our plan and added a little bit of Him as we saw fit. How in the world do any of us do this differently? All of our instincts lead us to ourselves first.

We were also looking for an enemy, someone to blame, someone to fight, or a dragon to slay. Many people with cancer personify their disease to give it a face or set of traits to better visualize their fight. By making the disease into someone or something, the diagnosed believe they can somehow contain it, reason with it or simply defeat it. I think these are all valuable tools for people facing their cancer, and I would not strip them of this mental tool or resource.

For me however, I recognize that cancer is just a part of a broken world. This is not a world that God envisioned when He created the Garden of Eden, nor is it a world He wants me to live in now. Because of the fall, sin and death entered into our world, and there are consequences for that. One of those consequences is cancer, often leading to death. Do I fight those consequences? You bet I do! Does God want to lead me in this fight, and does Jesus stand beside me and ask me to lean on Him through this struggle? You bet He does! Do I know how this ends . . . yes, with me in heaven; either from the cancer in the future, or from any one of a hundred things that will ultimately cause my death. We still have a 100% mortality rate on this planet, and nobody gets off this planet alive. In the end, a big part of this process is about attitude.

What is the right attitude for what appears to be catastrophic news?

a. Ignore it, and say, "this is not catastrophic, my God is an awesome God and He has this!" "This," while knowing full well that you are scared out of your mind, and really just want it to go away?

b. Embrace the catastrophe, and say, "This will be God's shining moment as He rescues one of His children with His incredible power, and earns glory for Himself (and me) in the process?"

c. Wait and watch, hoping that it is not really a catastrophe, but rather a small blip that some medication will address so we can get back to the "normal" of worshiping and loving God?

d. Prepare for the inevitable with a brave face, so that people will remember you as faith filled and a strong witness until the bitter end?

e. Go out in a blaze of glory with trips, treasures, and toys so that you leave no bucket list item unchecked?

f. Hole up, become depressed, and live out the remaining time with one eye to the clock and the other picking out funeral songs and verses?

g. All of the above in various amounts and measures as the days pass as both the prognosis improves and conversely, setbacks occur?

Standing up versus looking up

On my tippy toes, at the height of my own perceived suffering or potential suffering, I could not reach the foot of the cross. However, in my broken state, on my knees groveling in the tears, sweat and blood of my Savior at the foot of his victory perch, I could see Him clearly. We met when I stopped trying to stand up and manage my condition myself, but instead looked up and begged for His help.

We had a very sober and honest conversation, Jesus and me. We talked about my definition of catastrophic. We talked about my fears and objections to departing this world prematurely. We talked about my concerns for those that I would leave behind. We talked about my treatment options and the wealth of inspired, but human developed cures, and where I should place my hope. We talked a lot, with Him on the cross, and me on my knees. I felt His words more than I heard them, and they were like stirrings in my memory, because they had already been presented to me in His word in different forms over years.

Here is what He said to me:

- *Be still and know that I am God.* Be at peace, and remember that I have not only this situation, but all of space, time, and matter in my control. What is cancer to me? It is but a small thing, of little regard in my plan. It is large to you now, but in your eternal life that began at your conception, it is but a millisecond. Relax, let it go, let me take care of this in my way, and on my schedule. I am the Alpha and the Omega, the beginning and the end. You have had a beginning, but in me you will have no end.

- *I have overcome the world.* Your condition is one of sin created at The Fall, but removed through my blood. Cancer is of this world, but you are not. You are an alien here, destined to return to your true home with me. Please do not worry about the world, or your family, or the things of your daily life. All of these have been placed by my Father under my feet, and I will take care of my own as I always have, in my way, and in ways that give my Father glory.

- *Whether by your living or your dying.* Your life is not your own, it is mine; and I purchased it at a heavy price, because it was worth a heavy price. I will not throw it away, or deal with it carelessly. However, your life's purpose on earth is to lead others to me. You have no other purpose . . . PERIOD. It is mine to judge whether your recovery, or a painful journey, will most effectively maximize that purpose. Your worrying and efforts will not impact my will, so stop trying. Continue to ask for the strength to endure in all things, and I have promised I will give it to you.

- *All things work to His glory for those who love Him.* Nothing is an accident in my universe. Not a leaf falls, or a drop of water moves, that I do not know about it. All things seen, and unseen, including your cancer, ultimately work to God's glory. If you truly love me, you will see that the outcome of treatment is completely relevant to my plan, regardless of what it is. I will use this to bring glory to my Father, and you will be an instrument of that. Be grateful for the chance to serve His will, and be watchful for the miracles in your life that further that will.

- *New measures of grace every day.* When you learned of your cancer, that was my grace. When you discovered the genetic mutation that could be treated with directed

111

therapy, that was my grace. When you found out that you had not one, but three therapies, that were expensive but would be covered 100% by your insurance; that was my grace. Every morning that you breathe without effort, is a mercy; and in the future, every breath that you fight through is also my mercy.

Our conversations have, and continue to provide, the "peace that surpasses all understanding." People comment all the time on my attitude, and occasionally imply that I am in denial. In some ways, I am in denial. I actively deny that cancer or death have any power over me. I actively deny that my faith will be challenged, or diminished, but will only be increased through the presence of Jesus as my partner in my struggle. I actively deny that the devil's great tools of fear and misdirection will cause my gaze to waver or my energy to flicker in my pursuit of witnessing about Jesus. I think people are right, and denial is a good thing!

So how about those doctors?

Fifteen (15) months before I was diagnosed, I had a chest scan to detect calcification on the major arteries going to and from the heart. My twin brother had just had a heart attack and I wanted to know if I had any blockages. During that scan, a small nodule had been detected on the lower left lobe of my lung. Detected, but not highlighted or separately reported to either myself or my regular physician, this report went into my file to be stored for a little while.

Fast-forward 15 months later, to my annual physical. An interesting conversation takes place. My previous doctor had retired. I had a newly assigned physician. The computers had just gone through a major system change and he was putting in all my history, by hand, into a new record keeping system as we went through my file. This meant he had to go through literally 20 years of history with me, on a page-by-page basis, and pick and choose what was worth adding to the database. About one half hour in, we get to this little gem:

Dr. B: "So whatever happened with the nodule that was detected earlier last year on your lung?"

Tim: "What nodule?"

Dr. B: "The nodule that they found when they did your heart scan."

Tim: "Nobody told me about a nodule, I have no idea."

Dr. B: "Well it is probably nothing, but I am going to ask for a CT scan just to be sure. This is what happens when you are a general practitioner like me. The folks doing the scan only care about the heart and the heart concerns that you were asking about, they make no notes about the other discoveries. This kind of information just gets sent over, put in your file, and ignored, until someone like me has to update your full history."

This little interchange led to an ultimate diagnosis of lung cancer. But hold on a second, you might say . . . what about the negligence of the hospital, or the laboratory, or the person that put the report into your file? What about all that, and lawsuits, or accountability, or just plain old outrage at the incompetence of the medical community? Where is your sense of justice? God had a plan for me on this front as well.

Never got there. Not even for a minute. Neither did my wife or my family. Not because we are great Christians, or that we easily forgive. Nope, the rest of the story showed to us the awesome wisdom of God, and we marveled that He had this play out in the way that it did.

See, if I had been diagnosed at the time of the original scan, it is likely that I would be dead. My oncologist told me that the drugs that were capable of treating my extremely rare form of cancer had only been approved for use a few months previously. If my cancer had been discovered "on time," they would have started an aggressive chemotherapy regimen. My prognosis would have been only a year or so to live. However, because I only became symptomatic and had the real diagnosis at this time, instead of the year earlier, I would be eligible for the easy to take, low side effect medication. This new medication had an 80% chance of putting the cancer into remission within 12-16 weeks. We recognized in that moment, that God really does have the power and control. His understanding of the right time is the only understanding that matters!

Fast-forward six weeks. I am in my follow up appointment with the cardiologist that had reviewed my original heart scan. He had reviewed my chart and knew that I had lung cancer. We had a very different conversation than my meeting with my family doctor:

Dr. P: "How did they discover you had cancer?"

Tim: "During my annual physical, my new physician was entering all my pertinent life stage information and came across my heart scan that had the 2.5 cm nodule in it, and asked for a follow up scan."

Dr. P: "Hmmm, I see that, and I see that the nodule actually made it to my notes for our follow up meeting over a year ago. Hmmmm . . . . [Significant Pause]. Tim, I am so sorry. It is in my notes, but I never made it part of a plan. I am so sorry that you went this long without a diagnosis. I am horrified for the part I played in the failure of the system to detect this earlier, I am very sorry."

Tim: "Doctor, it is just fine. This is a 'God's hand' kind of thing. If I had been diagnosed at the time, I would have gone through chemo instead of directed therapy, and very likely I would not be here."

Dr. P: "I am so sorry"

Tim: "Doctor, I forgive you, and there is nothing that can be done now except to learn whatever you can from this moment. In the meantime, I am not angry, or upset, and I am certainly not going to sue you or this hospital. This is God's will, and it is to His glory that I can tell you that."

Dr. P: "Thank you for what you said, I really appreciate it. I will be praying for you."

What about the rest of the world?

For those of you that don't have cancer, I simply say, "Great, but what else has you on your knees, or should?" It is fair to say that the world knocks us down, and although our instinct is to get up, we need only to look up. From your knees, you will be amazingly in touch with the source of all power. Power is what you will need to face whatever catastrophe you are addressing.

Let's fast-forward another six weeks, to about 3 months since the diagnosis. I visit my oncologist, and he lets me know that I am in remission. That's right . . . no cancer can be seen on my scans. That was the exact prayer that we had been praying since I was first diagnosed. I had been using the possibility of remission as the "holding my breath," point from which all other future lines of hope or acceptance would begin. Again, God had blessed me with clarity, and a great answer, and a wink to tell me that He had this all along. But what if I had not received good news? What then? I pray now that my response would have been similar . . .gratitude and wonder.

I don't kid myself that cancer and I are done. It is unlikely that I will be declared cured, and my oncologist has told me that. However, I keep praying in full knowledge that someday, something is going to be the death of me, and start my re-birth in heaven. Having stared this one in the eye, I am more confident that with God's help, it will be easier next time.

Whoa there, brave man! That sounded pretty good, like your faith was all set. When we got to fast-forward again to seven weeks later, I found out that I was no longer in remission. My cancer was back, and although the nodule had not reformed, and the lymph nodes were still invisible; the telltale cells had re-emerged.

What did we do? We did what we always do . . .we fled! We went to New Orleans and ran from the fear, the truth, and the future as hard as we could. It is hard when "the hits just keep coming," and we keep managing the radio stations playing in our mind. Somewhere between the station of fear and the one of trust, comes a clear signal that we can hold on to. Unfortunately, we know that both stations play at high volume. We have to constantly decide which one we are going to listen to.

Every time I think this cancer thing makes sense, I get hit with a new revelation. I am not in remission, but I am in treatment. My treatment is experimental, so I have anywhere from one year to "we really don't know how long" to live. So, I stay on my knees and do the work that God places in front of me.

What has you on your knees in prayer?

- Is it loss? The loss of a job, a loved one, or your sense of self-worth?
- Is it betrayal? Infidelity, broken friendships, or the promise of a future that has been taken away?
- Is it your fear of things beyond your control? Your children, your parents, your own mortality, or certainty?

Regardless of the cause, the effect is the same from prayer. On our knees, we know that we have tapped into the power that will make change, heal wounds, right wrongs and save lives. We also know that from this position, we are promised peace. That's right, peace, but not a solution we will immediately understand. We can possess the emotional comfort to know an answer is coming, and it is being spoken with the voice that created everything.

Sometimes when I am on my knees, I am also shaking my head and smiling in wonder. In spite of the fear, and in addition to the surrender, I have this tremendous sense of awe. God has knitted the universe together in such a way that all these pieces could fall into place in a way that not only my medical situation could be managed, but that my family could clearly see His hand and testify to His awesome power. And that is just for me, 1 in almost 7 billion people on a speck of dust, in the backwater of His creation. UNBELIEVABLE! That's right, I would not believe it if I had not lived it myself, and heard the whispers of truth as I spoke with Him . . . on my knees and looking up.

<u>Chapter 8 Summary</u>

Key Points:

- God is not the cause of our pain or troubles.
- We cannot see God properly when we approach Him standing up and full of our own certainty.
- Each challenge that the world puts in our path, is an opportunity to witness to the redeeming love and grace of Jesus Christ.

Key Questions:

- What should have you on your knees now?
- What has those around you on their knees, and how can you join them at the foot of the cross?
- Where can you see God's mercy in the pain and challenges that the fallen world has dealt you?

Prayer:

Lord Jesus Christ, son of the Living God, I am in awe of your power, your wisdom, your strength and your love for me. You sacrificed yourself so that I would never have to fear death and could always look forward to eternity with you. Forgive my fear, and continue to open my eyes to your work all around me;

that I may give glory to you in all circumstances and to each person I meet. In your precious name. Amen.

Chapter 9: Guilt Is Not Just for Mothers

"Happy is the person whose sins are forgiven, whose wrongs are pardoned. Happy is the person whom the Lord does not consider guilty and in whom there is nothing false. When I kept things to myself, I felt weak deep inside me. I moaned all day long. Day and night you punished me. My strength was gone as in the summer heat. Then I confessed my sins to you and didn't hide my guilt. I said, I will confess my sins to the Lord, and you forgave my guilt."

Psalm 32:1-5 (NCV)

Parents are great, and I have been told so by my parents since I was very little. My folks told me that someday I would grow up to be just like them . . . and I have. They told me that I would grow up to have kids just like me . . . and I have. My mother told me that someday I would write a book, and inside I could put all the things that they taught me . . . and I have.

Parents say a lot of things when we are little, and we learn that a lot of what they tell us is right, much later.

Recently, I have been doing some odd jobs for my folks around their house. The fact that I have picked up some "honey do's" for them is odd enough all by itself. However, add in the fact that I and my parents experience déjà vu . . . hearing their voices back in my youth and the constant inspection as I do the work . . . and you have a recipe for hysteria. Having my mother watch me as I work, is the equivalent of people watching you through the windshield as you squeegee the glass on a car. It is a little nerve wracking and the inspection is right in your face.

At brunch, prior to going over to their house for an hour or so of fun, I casually made the comment, "I hope that today does not involve vacuuming all the floors again." Sure, this was a passive aggressive shot across the formidable bow of mom's "to do" list, but it was worth a try. Her response was classic! "Well, if you don't mind seeing all those little things on the wood floor, I guess we can live with them too." As you would expect, I had been one-upped by the master of guilt. My response to my mother was to point out, "I don't know if I have heard a clearer use of guilt from you in a long time!" To which she smiled and said, "Well if you want to stay in fighting trim, you have to practice."

Guilt is a masterful application of a concept called leverage. "Give me a **lever long enough** and a fulcrum on which to place it, and I shall **move** the **world**." A dead Greek guy named Archimedes said that, and it was about the application of leverage. Leverage is wonderful, because it allows someone to effect large change with minimal effort. Guilt is one of the great levers that move people all the time. Even better, it does not require too much work to get its job accomplished.

Guilt is a pervasive obstacle to grace.

There are two kinds of guilt; the guilt for what we have done or will do, and the guilt for what we have not done or know that we will not do. In shorthand, the guilt of action and the guilt of inaction. The Bible is full of guilt, which is why mothers of all ethnic and religious backgrounds use it so effectively . . . They have a training manual!

The guilt of action

Most of us use guilt every day in one way or another. We cajole and manipulate people to move in a direction that we desire, and guilt is just another tool in our toolbox to accomplish what we want. It is possible that your spouse, kids or coworkers can spot you using guilt to effect change, and you may not even see it. Some people call this being passive aggressive. This approach involves you using a stated or implied acceptance of something that is counter to your will, but with an easily understood hint of judgment that the choice or behavior is unacceptable. We say yes, but everything about our behavior and language implies we are disappointed. Guilt is our tool of last resort when something is not going to go our way, or our first choice, when we suspect that it won't.

We may mistakenly believe that God uses guilt as well. God does not use guilt, because the very nature of guilt implies it has to be used as a manipulative tool to accomplish an end. What God allows to seep into our being is shame. Shame is different than guilt. Shame is a similar emotional response to guilt, but instead of the very human leverage of failed expectations, shame is the real response to God's standard and our unwillingness to even attempt to live to that standard.

But, the guilt we feel for how we wrong each other pales in comparison to the shame felt by Christians when we recognize that we have wronged God. In some ways, it might be easy to ignore our shame with God. As a spiritual being, we don't have to face Him eye to eye and admit our mistakes. God is all forgiving, which is a real plus when you know that you will sin again. But in the quiet recesses of our minds, where we still admit right and wrong without equivocation or justification, God sits patiently. He is waiting for us to face the truth; we screwed up again.

Shame is useful. Shame helps us return to our Father in heaven, and seek forgiveness, guidance and assistance. Shame is our appropriate response to a perfect God in the face of an imperfect self. Shame is our reflection in the mirror that Jesus holds up to ask our response to His judgment, just prior to His sharing of grace. Shame does not get in the way of grace, it should rather be the emotion just prior to the regular acceptance of the joyous gift of grace. It is in spite of our failures and shame for them, that Christ gave us grace.

Guilt is created because we think we got away with something, and then we got caught. Guilt is our sinful response to our sinful action, when we know that we should have turned to God's will, but chose a different path instead. Guilt is how we feel when we have pretended that we are in a moral dilemma and went sideways. Guilt is our response when we sin against others. Guilt is the good part of our created being responding to the actions of the fallen inside each of us. Guilt is a lot of things . . .it is very, very busy in our lives!

Our words, thoughts and actions are sinful; shame is our spiritual response to God, while guilt is our emotional response when we know we have done wrong.

Why is guilt so bad? Guilt gets in the way of understanding grace. Here is how the cycle goes. Sin leads to guilt, guilt leads to anger, and anger leads to greater sin.

Sin leads to guilt. When we harm another, the response described before kicks in, and we are knee deep in guilt before we know it. This can be a physical response including cold sweats, sleepless nights, and tears. When we attempt to resolve guilt in a productive manner, we can follow a straightforward pattern with other people.

- Admit the wrong we have committed without equivocation, rationalization, or an attempt to share blame.
- Repent of our failure.
- Ask for forgiveness.
- Express gratitude.
- Move forward.

At times, my anger has neither been righteous nor proportional. I have gotten "white hot" at what is a small matter and become irrational in my response. I have yelled, swore, or completely shut down in exchanges with my wife or kids. Even time with professionals has not isolated all the triggers that create this emotional tirade. It is way, way out of line. In this fury, I am sin embodied, unchecked, unbending, and unrepentant . . . and then the storm passes, and I am left with the detritus of a terrible shipwreck, with survivors desperately trying to find safety. Over time, I have come to learn a great deal about the dark part of myself that I fight during these moments.

I have learned to work through the pattern, and to seek the forgiveness of those I hurt. Having a pattern for resolution has not only helped me move past the guilt, but actually to learn the many things I have to do to avoid the creation of the need for forgiveness in the first place. But for the longest time, I Idid not resolve my guilt over my misspent anger, and instead let it drive further anger.

Guilt can be resolved . . . or it cannot be. When we do not face our sin, acknowledge it, and repent of it, it gets worse. It is an established Biblical principle that sin begets sin. Simply put, when we start sinning, our ongoing effort to cover up or hide from our sin will cause us to sin more.

When we don't face our sin, and guilt springs up inside of us, this emotion cannot go unaddressed. Guilt gnaws, paws, pants and begs to be let loose from within us. Guilt does not have a healthy cage inside of us, so it demands to be set free. However, if it is not going to be released through the redemptive process, it will demand to be fed. Like anything that is wild and caged, it will become angry until it is heard. This unresolved guilt takes on a life of its own which leads to anger.

What is this anger? If we cannot bring ourselves to repent of our sin, we try to make it seem like it is no longer sin. How do we make sin into not sin? Through our righteous anger and indignation of course! In short, we claim our sin is a fair and measured response to something that has been done to us. By blaming others for the impetus for our sin, we hope to absolve ourselves of the first sin. It is the five-year old in us that says, "If he had not taken my truck, I would not have had to hit him. He deserved it!"

When we can rationalize our sin, we are now capable of stoking our fires of anger to further invest in a cycle of retribution. If our guilt is substantial, our corresponding anger has to be large enough to not only cover the first sin, but what must be done next. When we sin against someone, if they do not forgive us, even without the redemptive cycle; it is likely we have started an arms race of anger and sin between us. A lie requires a bigger lie, or series of lies, to cover for it. A wrong requires another and another to balance the scale between us and the party in question. Sin begets sin, and so the cycle continues.

Has someone ever sinned against you and because of that you resented them, you took action against them? Have you ever done something that had intended or unintended consequences that caused you to feel guilt? Have you seen where that unresolved guilt has taken you?

The guilt of inaction

Oh, it is subtle, and we become desensitized to it, but the sin of inaction is probably more present for me than the other one. The homeless person on the street with a cup and a sign rarely gets a second look any more. The world relief agencies with their television ads and requests for help and aid get a fast forward on my DVR. The friend in the hospital on Friday night gets a little consideration, but no meaningful help or succor from me. The stranger in clear need at the gas station, rest stop, corner, or anywhere else gets little attention, but often a look of knowing judgment as I hurry by.

Jesus told me in Matthew how I was supposed to behave:

"For I was hungry and you gave me something to eat, I was thirsty and you gave me something to drink, I was a stranger and you invited me in, I needed clothes and you clothed me, I was sick and you looked after me, I was in prison and you came to visit me." Then the righteous will answer him, Lord, when did we see you hungry and feed you, or thirsty and give you something to drink? When did we see you a stranger and invite you in, or needing clothes and clothe you? When did we see you sick or in prison and go to visit you? "The King will reply, "Truly I tell you, whatever you did for one of the least of these brothers and sisters of mine, you did for me."

Matthew 25:35-40 (NIV)

I guess I cannot pretend I don't know who they are, these 'least of my brothers'. And I see them . . .these least of my brothers and sisters. They are with me regularly and they are not hiding. I don't have to wonder if God is putting those in need in my path, I have to step over them literally and figuratively to get just about everywhere I go. Maybe some of the questions below will feel familiar:

- Is it my self-justification? I don't know if I stopped caring, or if I am just indifferent due to my focus on my own problems. I have lots of things that are in my mission field, and I am doing a lot, so doing more for a new or different group does not seem to work. What about the fact that "I hear that the panhandlers are all organized, make a lot of money doing this, and it all goes to organized crime or to drugs?"

- Is it my selfishness? Lots of the things I should do require time, money or effort. I have given to my church, my family, and my job, isn't that enough? What is enough? If I give to one group or another, am I not slighting everyone else? How do I decide which group is worthy? I have my own needs and my family to take care of, and at some point, enough is enough!

- Is it my lack of compassion? The story of the good Samaritan goes a long way toward describing who my brother is, but honestly, if he doesn't look like me, or doesn't really seem worthy, why would I waste anything on him? Aren't there others that are worse off, and if I don't have anything to give the 'even worse off' group, how can I give to this person that is only in a really bad way?

Do I feel guilty? Sure. As a matter of fact, I hear a lot of things in my head as I go about the not helping the least of my brothers. My head is so full of thought, that there is no room left for generosity. I am very engaged in describing to myself why it is okay not to act or care.

Possibly from time to time, I give a little change to a homeless person. Maybe I feel compelled to donate to a charity that a friend is supporting. I am okay with making a donation in cash that will not put me on some list that gets passed around or worse, sold to other groups who can in turn hit me up for more money. But let's keep the investment transactional and untraceable, lest people come to expect this level of giving at some point in the future. I like the exchange of a few dollars for a good feeling, but no real commitment.

Jesus does not see it the same way I do. As a matter of fact, through the Biblical writers He tells us to:

- Care for others.
- Bind up the wounded.
- Visit the lonely and in prison.
- Take care of the widows and orphans.
- Give more than we are asked.

Similar to the guilt of action, when faced with the standard of Jesus, my guilt of inaction turns to shame. Of course, this happens to me only "when faced with the standard of Jesus." Without His word, His story, His instructions, I might have only a nagging sense of guilt that would ultimately go away. It is through the stark contrast of my own sinfulness, measured against the full magnitude of His grace, that I understand the gap I have created.

It must be an incredible trick of the devil, or our fall, that we forget the pleasure that comes from giving unselfishly to others. I cannot recall a time that, in a moment of inspiration, I gave to someone with no thought to myself that it did not feel great! Survey after survey points to an amazingly positive set of outcomes for the giver as much as the receiver; when giving is done anonymously, generously and frequently. What keeps us surrounded by our own failure, and therefore, the guilt and ultimately shame that accompany it?

In a country that has known mostly abundance throughout its history, we are terrified of scarcity. The questions we ask ourselves at the inflection point of someone else's need are small minded and weak. We face the query in our head about all of our resources: Will I have enough? Will I have enough in case my spouse loses his or her job? What about for college, retirement, the upcoming wedding, or other essentials? Will I have enough for the lifestyle I have always hoped for? These nagging questions get into our mind and become the lens through which we view each opportunity. The ultimate question becomes, "If I give to him/her/them, will I have enough for me?"

Of course, the fear of not having enough is rooted in our lack of trust in God. We think about our need as if God is unaware of what daily bread we require. Worse, we are convinced that if left to His own devices (meaning without our efforts), He would not let us have all the things that we want. This tension exists as though we are playing tug of war between our hard work, and God's interest in having us live in poverty. At times, we might comically think that our success is our own, and not really a gift from Him.

It is more than okay to be generous. Our God is the master of "more than enough." He not only provides the daily bread we pray for, He showers us with a great deal more, so that we can show His love through our choice to share. Guilt and shame need not be our motivation when joy is so much more meaningful!

Chapter 9 Summary

Key Points:

- Guilt is a sinful tool that is used by us or on us to manipulate.
- Shame is an acknowledgment of how far short of the standard of Jesus we fall.
- Guilt through inaction is still guilt, and must be replaced with generosity.

Key Questions:

- What makes you feel guilty?
- Are there places in which you are using guilt as a tool out of habit or perceived need, to get your way that you can eliminate?
- Do you feel shame, and can you identify the part of your life that is farthest from the standard of Jesus?

Prayer:

Lord, you have given me so much. I know that you ask me to act out of love and compassion, and to seek opportunities to be generous, but I let fear and selfishness get in my way. Forgive my efforts to limit your greatness in my thoughts, or to direct my own future through storing, when I should be sharing. Release me today from my shame, and replace it with greater trust in your grace. I beg you to replace the guilt I feel and the guilt I impose on others with love, wisdom and a giving heart. I ask these things in your son's name. Amen.

Chapter 10: Everyone's an Addict

"Do not love the world or anything in the world. If anyone loves the world, love for the Father is not in them. For everything in the world—the lust of the flesh, the lust of the eyes, and the pride of life—comes not from the Father but from the world. The world and its desires pass away, but whoever does the will of God lives forever."

1 John 2: 15-17 (NIV)

"My name is Tim, and I am an alcoholic." In response to this statement, a chorus of "Hi, Tim!" will go up if you are at an addict meeting. I have only been to one meeting, but I can assure you that this well-known exchange takes place. I have been told that it is not reserved for Alcoholics Anonymous; but for every group meeting which addresses, in a safe and sober setting, the issues of addiction.

I wonder why we don't have more "_____ Anonymous" groups out there for the many addictions beyond alcohol, drugs, sex and gambling? We are all addicted to something. Truly. Most people do not think of themselves as being addicted, but within a few minutes of conversation, you can find the something that they could not live without and might even do unthinkable things to keep or accumulate more of. Maybe we have such a stigma around the word addiction that we cannot even properly think about it.

A new definition of addiction should be employed. In the traditional definition, the emphasis is on the item deemed to be causing the addiction. Under a new definition, the emphasis would no longer be upon the source of addiction or even the cause, but upon the negative outcome it creates. Maybe it would be something like this, "Whatever habitually and incessantly gets between us and the grace that God wants us to enjoy, that only His great power will be able to remove."

People say that alcohol makes them evil, or drugs turn them bad. This is not true. Sobriety often holds back the evil that is harbored in our heart all the time. For me, alcohol did not remove my inhibitions, it removed my good sense and unleashed the unfiltered and unmanageable sinner that is inside of me. My vicious tongue, my judgmental commentary, my willingness to treat others poorly, are all held at bay by sobriety. Alcohol did not turn me evil, it released more of my evil thoughts and actions. What causes us to behave in an evil manner? We are sinful by nature, and believe me that is enough!

Addiction is an obstacle to receiving God's grace.

We all want the easy. The addict gets caught up in the pursuit of what looks like the easy way to . . . escape, happiness, a different life, a release from earthly bonds, or the mundane. When we seek easy on our own, it comes with a low price for a while. However, the nature of addiction is that more of the same thing is required to achieve the same feeling that was easy before. On our journey to get more of this feeling, we leave many things along the roadside. My friend Tony Harrison says it this way, "Addiction will take you places you don't want to go, for longer than you want to stay, at a price that is higher than you want to pay."

But isn't grace easy? Shouldn't grace be the easy that we long for? It would make sense, because if the easy out was what we were really looking for, nothing is easier than free. If the price for addiction is high, and climbs the longer we move along the path, why wouldn't we give up the ever-harder answer? The addict has an answer, and if you know an addict, you know that we have an answer for everything! The answer is that the feeling is not the same, or the high is not as high, or that we just can't stop now that we are in so deep, no matter how hard we try. We know what the Psalmist says, and we reject it outright.

"For God alone, O my soul, wait in silence,
for my hope is from Him.

He only is my rock and my salvation,
my fortress; I shall not be shaken.

On God rests my salvation and my glory;
my mighty rock, my refuge is God.

Trust in Him at all times, O people;
pour out your heart before Him;
God is a refuge for us."

Psalm 62: 5-8 (ESV)

For the addict, a simple replacement throughout the Psalm of their addiction in place of God would be appropriate. In my case, I would insert alcohol. Think about how this sounds now:

For alcohol alone, O my soul, wait in silence,
for my hope is from it.

Alcohol only is my rock and my salvation,
my fortress; I shall not be shaken.

On alcohol rests my salvation and my glory;
my mighty rock, my refuge is alcohol.

Trust in alcohol at all times, O people;
pour out your heart before it;
Alcohol is a refuge for us.

This is the way that addiction looks and feels to the addict. All thought moves to the next opportunity to be with the thing that we are addicted to. It is perceived as the source of strength and hope. It is the salvation, and we pour our heart out before it.

But that cannot be you, can it? I mean for druggies, booze hounds and perverts that are porn or sex addicts, this description may make sense; but what about the everyday person? More importantly, what about for Christians? What could they possibly be addicted to, that they would replace God with something else on a daily basis? Surely, they do not suffer from these delusional relationships?

A friend of mine was doing a construction review of the plans for a Hindu temple and came across something curious. In the basement, was a room that was simply entitled, "Deity Storage." We had a pretty good laugh about what it means to have so many gods that you actually have to have a storage location for the statues. With a single god which has as many as 10 million manifestations, it must be hard to keep up with who is having a holiday, or which embodiment deserves worship this week.

I wondered however, where do we store our gods? Oh, I don't mean the Trinity, but instead, the things we treat as gods. What things do you treat as more important than your relationship with God? We have all heard the sermons extolling the virtues of putting God first, and the risk and penalties we experience if we move him down the list. However, all of us are addicted to something that places God somewhere other than the top of the list. Below is a list of potential addictions for you. This may not be exhaustive, but it is likely that you are addicted to, or in recovery from, at least one of these. Which one(s) fit for you?

Substances - Anything that you can put into your system. Tobacco, alcohol, prescription painkillers, illicit materials like cocaine, heroin, and others . . .they are all by their very nature addictive. By design, they are built to create reliance in your mind and body, and will require that more be used over time.

Risk - Whether it is gambling, skydiving, fast driving, cheating on a spouse, thievery of any kind, or any other adrenaline triggering experience, risk is addictive. People talk about the thrill of taking risks, but what about the costs of what the risk addiction takes from you? Over time, nobody wins 100% of the time, and the thrill would not exist if consequences were not the alternative outcome.

Sexual gratification - Pornography, sex outside of marriage, risky behaviors, exploring alternative lifestyles, and anything that focuses on the act of sex rather than the purpose for sex can easily become addictive. Sex was created so that a married man and a woman can create a family and enjoy each other's company in the way that they were intended.

Power - Springsteen said it best in his song, Badlands:

> "Poor man wanna be rich
>
> Rich man wanna be king
>
> And a king ain't satisfied
>
> 'Til he rules everything"

Success is measured not just by where you come from, but also how much farther you have to go to get to the next step.

Sports - You can watch them or play them. You can cheer one sport or every sport. You can have a team, or an entire league, but if your time is spent mostly on sports channels, fantasy teams, and watching games, there is a good chance that this hobby has become more than that.

Health - Workouts, health drinks, diets and the like are great! Our bodies are temples unto the Lord. However, if the creation (us) spends too much time refining the created (our bodies), we will lose sight of the importance of the creator (God). The pursuit of health is often a proxy for a hope that we can forestall death. We will work on ourselves until we know that we will outlast the average. This is sin, as well as folly, when we think we can determine what our length of days will be.

Money - It is not that money is the root of all evil. According to 1 Timothy 6:10 (ESV) "the *love of money* is a root of all kinds of evils. It is through this craving that some have wandered away from the faith and pierced themselves with many pangs." When we love our money, our wealth, our ability to purchase, and want more of it; we often allow our addiction to change our behaviors, and re-orient how we spend our time and exert ourselves towards its pursuit.

Lifestyle - I have many friends called Jones. I have never felt obligated to keep up with them, nor do I ask them to keep up with me. However, in the American lexicon, it appears that everyone wants to keep up with the Joneses. Clearly whomever these folks are, they have it all, and our lives fall shockingly short of theirs. You can never have enough of what you do not need. This means cars, clothes, boats, vacations, homes, etc.

are not going to ever be enough or good enough to fill the hole that we keep shoveling into.

Family - If family gets in the way of God, we have a problem. We make our children or our spouse into god for us when they displace Him in the priority scheme of our lives. This sounds terribly weird, but Jesus was clear on this in Luke 14:26 (KJV), "If any man come to me, and hate not his father, and mother, and wife, and children, and brethren, and sisters, yea, and his own life also, he cannot be my disciple."

Good works - Doing good, feels good. We can become so enamored with the feeling that we forget the reason. Sometimes the ministry becomes greater in our mind than why we do it. We do not do ministry because it feels good, we do it out of obedience; and from that obedience, the good feelings will naturally flow. Any time the outcome becomes more important than the purpose, we have put something in front of God.

Sin - Judgment, foul language, dark thoughts, manipulation, self-reliance and all other forms of opposition to the will of God including everything in the list before, get in our way of being

His children and accepting His grace. All of us are addicted to sin. We replace His will with our will, His priorities with our own, and what He would have for us with what we think we want. This is sin, and it is highly addictive.

Regardless of what it is, it is never going to be enough. The Psalmist reminds us,

"Sheol and Abaddon are never satisfied, and never satisfied are the eyes of man."

Psalm 27:20 (ESV)

How do you know that you are actually addicted? Is there a test that you can take to determine if it is addiction, or simply a healthy interest or a hobby? I found the following edited checklist by JR Thorpe, to be instructive in determining whether you have crossed the line into addiction:

1. You keep doing it even though there are clear negative consequences.
2. You suffer withdrawal if you attempt to stop.
3. You attempt to keep your use secret.
4. Your tolerance is increasing.

5. You can't seem to stop yourself.

6. You make excuses when other people act concerned.

7. You feel you need it to deal with your problems.

This works pretty well for assessing most of the substance-based addictions. But, it seems like a relatively poor list if we are applying it to the biggest addiction we all face, which is sin . . .or does it? Let's do a similar replacement to what we did with the Psalm before, and apply sin to this list, to see if a pattern does not become apparent.

1. *You keep sinning even though there are clear negative consequences.* We all have read that the "wages of sin is death." We know that sin begets sin, and that sin makes us miserable, separates us from God and others, and does not lead us to happiness. At a bare minimum, we can each check this box as a sign that we are addicted to sin.

2. *You suffer withdrawal if you attempt to stop sinning.* Can you imagine not sinning? Of course, you can! Each of us that has sinned, repented, sought and received forgiveness, imagines that they will not sin again in the same manner, until they do again! I don't know if it is withdrawal, because I don't

feel physically ill when I fail to sin, but something continues to draw me back into this cycle.

3. *You attempt to keep your sins a secret.* My beautiful daughter Ashton says that people most frequently pray the same prayer, "Lord, please don't watch me now!" Like Adam and Eve in the garden, we desperately try to hide or ignore our disobedience, hoping that the Lord or others won't see our sin. All sin comes with a label, "try to hide this if you can, otherwise, the consequences will probably be worse."

4. *Your level of sin is increasing.* As I get older, you would think I would sin less. As I study the Word, you would think I would sin less. As I engage in more Christian fellowship, you would think I would sin less. But I see my sin so much more clearly now, that it feels like I must be sinning more! God does not care about amount or severity of sin. As far as He is concerned, all sin and any sin will keep you from Him, without Jesus Christ. Although my sin may not be increasing, my awareness of it increases every day that I walk closer with Him.

5. *You can't seem to stop yourself.* Is sin unstoppable, or

insurmountable by human beings? Only one has ever done it, and that was Jesus Christ. Having said that, simply throwing up our hands and saying, "Well I guess it is human nature!" is not enough. Our effort to improve, in spite of our failings, is a form of obedience to His will. We cannot blot sin completely out of our lives, but we can make it a less controlling and dominant player in who we are, and what we do and think.

6. *You make excuses when other people act concerned about your sin.* I resent the heck out of anyone that observes my bad behavior and makes fun of or acts concerned about it. I think, "Who do they think they are to judge me? I know plenty of things about them that are equally as bad or worse than what they are telling me I am doing wrong!" Christian brothers and sisters that care enough to risk our relationship and attempt to guide me back to the path deserve my love, not my disdain.

7. *You feel you need to sin to deal with your problems.* When we do not feel God is enough for our problems, or we feel we cannot fully rely upon Him, we tend to move to our other gods to try to solve. Our impatience and lack of faith create a new sin in the form of not trusting God. If we trust God to deal with our problems, sin is not required.

As we re-run this list, it is hard not to feel as Paul did:

"Oh, what a miserable person I am! Who will free me from this life that is dominated by sin and death?"

Romans 7:24 (NLT)

Anything that is not God is doomed to fall short of our need. Jesus was speaking of more than physical or even spiritual nourishment when he was speaking to the woman at the well. Jesus said to her (and to us),

"Everyone who drinks of this water will be thirsty again, but whoever drinks of the water that I will give him will never be thirsty again. The water that I will give him will become in him a spring of water welling up to eternal life."

John 4:13-14 (ESV)

In essence, He said that all of our needs are met in Him, and none of our needs can be fully met apart from Him. We are made to only be satisfied in Jesus!

Every twelve-step program starts with the participant acknowledging the truth that they have a problem, and that the problem is bigger than they can solve alone. Some efforts have been made to further secularize these programs, but to little avail; as success in breaking the cycle of addiction truly requires the intervention of God. It is too big for us, and we will always revert to self-reliance and god replacement therapy to deal with our world until the Triune God becomes preeminent in our lives.

If you are addicted to a substance, risk or any of the items above for which professional help is appropriate, I urge you to seek it. If you are addicted to sin, or those private issues which may be only obvious to you, I urge you to seek spiritual help. The Word, prayer, community and meditation are all valuable means to address and remove those things that are replacing God as number one in your life.

Chapter 10 Summary

Key Points:

- Addiction is not simple, and everyone suffers from it.
- The thing that has become a larger portion or priority in our life than God, is what we are addicted to.
- Breaking the cycle of addiction requires more than we will ever be able to do alone.

Key Questions:

- What are you addicted to?
- How long have you tried to break the cycle of addiction to things that don't even appear sinful, and is it time to count on more than you alone?
- If you were no longer addicted, what would you replace that addiction with that would be God honoring?

Prayer:

I come to you in shame and torment Lord, as I realize I am not strong enough to face the thing that has replaced you as most important in my life. I am scared that it has control, and that you cannot or will not take it away. I cannot do this alone, and I don't want to even try any more. I ask you to enter my heart

and sweep away everything . . . big and small . . .seen and
unseen that gets in the way of you as most important in my life.
I ask this in your Son's name. Amen.

Chapter 11: God in the Silence

"My God, my God, why have you forsaken me?

Why are you so far from saving me, from the words of my

groaning?

O my God, I cry by day, but you do not answer,

and by night, but I find no rest."

Psalm 22: 1-2 (ESV)

For a couple of years, I worked with an intriguing young man named Michael. He had a young family and was a positive influence on everyone around him. I learned of his deep Christian faith and that he had felt called to become a missionary to Africa. He planned on taking his family for a several year assignment to share the message of the gospel in a small village. I was blown away by the story of his commitment to the mission field, and although I had heard about people like him, I had never met one. We had a chance to have some coffee, and I was anxious to learn more about his calling and his relationship with God.

During our conversation, I asked him if he felt called by God, and if so, if he felt that he actually "heard" God. He assured me that since he was a small child, he could feel and hear God speak to him every day. However, since the time when he had accepted God's command, he no longer heard God. I was astonished. I wanted to know why God might possibly choose to not to speak to his servant after he had faithfully accepted His will. Michael told me that he had come to rely on his special relationship with the Father, but that his faith had actually increased in His silence. Michael explained to me, "It takes very little faith to trust in God when He is speaking to you daily, but when you trust Him in His silence, your faith really grows."

Michael's story has made me consider some of the great patriarchs in the Bible, and what waiting must have been like for them. I have often thought about Abraham, of "the God of *Abraham*, Isaac and Jacob" fame. Ultimately, he becomes the father of many nations, but his story is a little spotty at best. He seems to have little regard for his beautiful wife, and regularly uses her to create situations from which he can profit. He is a contradiction in so many ways. His belief in the dream God gave him, of being the father to more people than the stars, was credited to him as righteousness. But his lack of trust in God's timing, which caused him to sleep with Hagar, is ultimately not counted against him.

During his life, his patience was repeatedly tested. He was told by God that he had a big role in the future, that he had been chosen, that he would be blessed and be a blessing. Looking at the timeline of this though, he clearly spent a lot of time scratching his head, trying to figure out when the good stuff would happen. Fifteen years after God made the promise that Abraham would have an heir, God had to reassure him that the promise was still coming. Even after that, it was ten more years before Sara gave birth to Isaac. That is a lot of waiting . . .and a lot of silence. Can we blame Abraham for being more than a little impatient?

Impatience is an obstacle to accepting God's grace.

It might astound us to know that God does not own a watch! See, we have watches, and He has time . . .all of time! He did not give Abraham the hope for a greater future to taunt him, but rather to give him hope. God shows us His will in a variety of ways that include signs, His word, insight through prayer, an inner attraction to something that truly feels right, and other ways. I will grant you that discerning the difference between His expression of His will, and my own inner desires can be tough to sort out, but it is there. Even the process of discernment will often take more time than we are willing to give it.

Why does God have us wait? Is He teasing us? Is it just an infinite game of "I know something you don't know?" Knowing the mind of God is the desire of every Christian. We are focused interminably on understanding Him. Albert Einstein said, "Show me God's thoughts. . .the rest are details." Asking why we wait is only one in a long list of questions that are on our minds. He has, however, given us some good guideposts in the lives of the people of the Bible for at least figuring out why He makes us wait.

Waiting may be hard for me because it requires a virtue I have misplaced . . .humility! If we are going to wait in the silence, we have to be humble enough to remember the entire time, that we are not in charge, and we don't make anything happen or will it into existence. True humility, for me, begins with a sheepish grin. I start by thinking how foolish I have been in trying to control something, and a bit of a wistful nod to God for reminding me that this is His show. I am a player on the stage to be directed, and I am to use a script that He has written.

One thing that God has always blessed me with is uncompromising hope. I did not say unwavering, just uncompromising. If but for the hope of hearing His voice, what would I do? Why would I want to go on? Once you have heard His voice, it is hard to imagine living your life without even the mere potential of hearing it again.

I have heard His voice in many places including my heart, apparent miraculous coincidence, an echo of a thought repeated through someone I trust, and in the world around me. Like Elijah in 1 Kings, He does not make a big thing about talking to me, He just makes certain that I have heard Him. But like an infomercial . . . "Wait there is more!" God is not always silent in my life.

- *God's presence.* Like many of you, I sense God in nature, the changing of the seasons, and in moments of conversation, where I just know that He is there. I sense something that cannot be of me, or experience Jesus actually in the room as He promised when two or more are gathered in His name. I get a jolt of the Holy Spirit who lives in my heart when something I am engaged in is "just what I am supposed to be doing." Yep, I feel God's presence even as I am typing these words. In these times I feel Him, and know the joy that He is there, but I admit I sometimes let the skeptic out of his cage and wonder if it is all just me. Strange that I can carry these two completely opposite thoughts in my head at the same time and not lose what is left of my mind!

- *God winks.* God winks are the best! This concept was captured and described in a book called . . . wait for it . . . "When God Winks". The book series walks through wonderful stories of apparent coincidences that are far too obviously created by the creator to be ascribed to random chance. For me, I have had God winks so many times that it is hard to pull just a few to use as examples. My favorite is the time I was driving, and a song came on the radio which inspired me to call my wife about a charity that we had not donated to in the past, but I felt called to at that time. Before I could even tell her what was on my mind, or an amount that had been placed on my heart, she started to tell me the exact same thing. No script, no plan, no reason that was obvious, but there was God winking as hard as He could at both of us!

- *God moments.* There are times when God catches me in His clarity, shakes me in His truth, and leaves me breathless in surprise. On four different occasions in my life, God has reached into my mind and heart at a pivotal point, and given me a clear understanding for His will for me. The best example may be from college. I had broken up with my long-time girlfriend and gotten involved in the seamier side of a lot of what college had to offer. On Valentine's Day, after two months of being apart, God woke me from a deep alcohol-induced slumber and showed me an "It's a Wonderful Life" type of choice for my life. I could clearly see where my life would go if I chose to continue my choice of debauchery, or if I returned to the path and gift He had given me. In this moment of clarity, I made two calls; one to make a break from my willful choice, and the other to beg to re-engage in the choice of His will. Over several months, my former girlfriend became my future wife. This was a

God moment, that had He not intervened, to my mind would not have happened.

God's presence, His winks, and His moments, strengthen my faith and calm my fears. They give me the hope to carry on when I do not think I can. The memory of these elements, of His mercy in touching a person like me is humbling, but they also create an enduring hope that more might be on the horizon.

But right now is not one of those times. Since my diagnosis of cancer, I have dealt with God in the silence. Certainly, the diagnosis has brought me closer to God as I seek Him and strive for Him, and beg Him, and study His Word. But I am getting no big or small revelations. I am in a rainforest valley surrounded by trees and undergrowth, and even the day is so dark from the foliage that I can barely make out the path in front of me. I am fearful of what night will bring in this lonely place, with no view, no companion, and no clear end to the journey. We hear of the Valley of Death, and assume that it is arid, hot and dusty. I can assure you that my valley is cloying and close and humid and full of life . . .so full of vibrant life around me that the thought of it causes me to be tearful. It feels like I will not be here that much longer, and I am clearly out of place in this strange world of overwhelming life. And have I mentioned how quiet it is in my valley? What does God want me to learn or prepare for in this silence?

Three kinds of preparation that God in the silence allows us to explore:

1. *God is preparing us.* Abraham had things to learn to be a father to nations. God knew his heart, his faithfulness, and his mind, and declared Abraham to be fit at the right time. Although not much is recorded in the Bible, clearly God used the 25 years to prepare Abraham. Like Abraham, we have things to learn, lessons to teach, and obstacles to struggle against and overcome through Him before we are ready; and it is God's time to reveal His will to us, or like Abraham, to make His revealed will become reality.

2. *God is preparing others.* From the time of the prophets, to the time of Christ, a great period of unusual silence existed between God and His people (about 430 years!) Although they would worship at the temple, and were engaged in what they believed to be his directives, they had no one that spoke for God to them that was authentic. Only when John the Baptist arrived did God again provide an oracle of what was about to come for

the people to listen to. In the meantime, some looked to His word, but the Pharisees and Sadducees looked to themselves and their own thoughts of right and wrong. In essence, their interpretation of God's will set them up as de facto God.

3. *God is preparing the way.* God is always at work, whether we can see His fingerprints or not. Isn't it amazing how many things come together, as if by luck, to make something important occur in our lives? It is always our choice to see serendipity or divinity. The unimaginable number of seemingly random occurrences; in the lives of your parents, grandparents and ancestors through time, that had to come together just right to create you, is mind-boggling. God's plan is fulfilled through circumstances that He has prepared, and sometimes time is what He requires to make the way ready.

Ok, so this picture of a silent God may be interesting, but what if I just can't wait? What if I believe the best thing I can do is get busy, and God will either catch up or bless my efforts along the way? What about the old (non-Biblical) saying, that "God helps those that help themselves?"

When our impatience gets the best of us, some not great things happen. We make plans, invest in efforts and work. We jump the gun of God, and then we are surprised that His plan is not revealed as we expected. Clearly, we have decided to replace the agent of all change with one of His lesser vessels, ourselves, and we hope for the same outcome. As my pastor reminds us, "Who is doing the doing?" Any time we replace the subject of the doing with ourselves instead of God, we are going to get it wrong!

Our potential response to waiting:

- *Preparation.* As referenced above, we can see waiting as merely preparation, and therefore a gift from God. We can prepare ourselves, prepare others, and we can prepare the way.

- *Prayer.* So many books, sermons and conversations have been had about both the form and value of prayer, that it seems silly to repeat all of it here. However, I believe that sometimes prayer is the most important and underrated activity we can engage in during God's apparent silence. Prayer is our opportunity to share our fears and at the same time, our hope and our trust. We must believe that trusting God is merited. He has been faithful in our lives in the past, or it would be unlikely that we would consider Him as capable of being faithful now or in the future. We have to lean into His faithfulness with prayers of trust and dependence to survive our own fears and doubts.

- *Vigilance.* If God is good all the time, then what are we sweating about? Two of God's faithful servants were vigilant, and patiently waited for the Messiah. Simeon, who had been told by the Holy Spirit that he would not die before he had seen the Lord's Christ; and Anna, who never left the temple, but worshipped night and day (Luke 2:21-38). Their vigilance was rewarded when one day a humble carpenter and his very young bride entered the temple and they met the Prince of the Universe. Like the story of the bridegroom and the ladies in waiting, these servants were prepared at any moment for the object of all affection to arrive and to take them into the ultimate banquet with him. They were vigilant and hopeful, as we must be.

Where is God apparently silent in your life now? Is it about a fear, a circumstance, or possibly a future outcome that appears uncertain? God will not be silent to you forever. He is well aware of our feeble hearts, and our need for His comforting voice. As Jesus said,

"My sheep hear my voice, and I know them, and they follow me."

John 10:27 (ESV)

His voice will return, but in the meantime, He is doing a great work in you through His silence. He is increasing your faith and challenging your impatience to become obedient to you and ultimately Him. The silence will become as nothing when you ultimately hear Him speak to you again.

Chapter 11 Summary

Key Points:

- God's silence is not God's absence.

- God has always known what He is doing, and when He will do it.

- Impatience is our human will trying to exert itself over God's will.

- There are good ways to use the time in the silence to prepare.

Key Questions:

- What are you waiting on that you have prayed for, that you are feeling God's silence?

- What steps are you taking that may place your will before His will?

- What can you do during this time of silence to prepare for when His will is revealed?

Prayer:

Lord, we are anxious all the time, praying and chasing, hoping and trying to fix. Forgive us our willful efforts to make our will into your will. Forgive us our efforts to force the outcomes that we have asked you for. Thank you for your silence as it increases our faith. We desperately want to hear your voice, but if silence is how you speak to us, please help us hear that with faith as well. We ask this in the name of Jesus, the Christ. Amen.

Chapter 12: Broken People Have Sharp Edges, and We Are All Broken

Will Rogers was quoted as saying, "I never met a man I didn't like." Of course, hundreds of bumper stickers have been made that identify one person or another that clearly Will did not run into. When I grew up in Nebraska, the bumper sticker was for the coach of our arch rival college football team, Oklahoma University, and the subject was Barry Switzer. Chevys, Fords, and Dodges would roll through the state of Nebraska proudly saying on the butt of their car, that "Will Rogers never met Barry Switzer." Inspiring! The implication was clear that even someone that can find something to like in everyone will find something to not like in at least one someone.

God loves broken people, but what choice does He have? We are all broken in some way. Whether it is through our own sinfulness, as a result of abuse, or what appears to be circumstance, we come to our relationship with Him in emotional and spiritual "pieces"; or maybe more clearly with pieces that have been broken off of us that need to be reattached, smoothed out or replaced. Our specific events or issues for brokenness are not the same. What breaks you may not break me, and vice versa. But in one sense we are all the same, we all need to be healed. We beg to be made whole.

It is actually easy to make an exhaustive list of the causes for brokenness, but my experience is that most people with a modicum of self-awareness can identify some of the sharp edges in their personality, outlook or judgment that highlight their own jaggedness. However, if I want a really good list of what the sharp edges are that poke them and prod them, I need only to ask them about anyone else's brokenness. Self-awareness in this area may be muted as an issue of emotional self-preservation but identifying the things that people do that cut me is natural.

I saw a meme in which Christian singer/songwriter Toby Mac declared, "*Everyone has a private battle they are facing which nobody knows about.*" In each person's poor behavior, we only see the symptoms, but not the source of their pain. If we were able to see the cause, it would be easier to understand and tolerate; but grace often involves treating broken people as if they are whole, without understanding anything about them. I know for myself, I would prefer to grant grace to people that seem to deserve grace, and not grant grace to the people that don't!

Waiting for someone to be grace worthy removes the possibility of giving them grace.

There is a very old joke that goes like this:

Q: How do porcupines mate?
A: VERY carefully!

People are a little like those porcupines. It is easy for us to be introduced, converse and even like each other, but that does not involve getting very close. Once real intimacy becomes likely, it is time to watch out for the sharp parts! I had an old boss that once said that you never really understood a person until you had driven in a car with them for eight hours or more. His point was that we can all be on our best behavior for a while, but nobody can hold back who they really are for too long.

There has always been a debate amongst sociologists concerning the nature of the mature individual. Was this person a product of their environment, and a summary of the experiences that happened to them? Or perhaps, the person was genetically predisposed from birth, to be the person we see today? This argument is often referred to as the nurture vs. nature debate. Many non-academics look at the two sides and conclude that it must be a combination of both. But for the Christian, it is the biology we were born with, coupled with the world we were placed in on purpose, and all of it bathed in the wonderful divine providence of a benevolent and wonderful God. We see our lives as having a grand design to them. More importantly, when we think of someone other than ourselves, we will or should think of their lives as having a grand design as well!

"I praise you, for I am fearfully and wonderfully made.
Wonderful are your works;
my soul knows it very well."

Psalm 139:14 (ESV)

Then why are people such jerks? Me especially! Most people I know don't really like big chunks of who they are, and the roughly 112,000 therapists in the United States (isn't Google amazing?) make most of their money on this fact! The psalmist understood both sides of the coin very well. Fearfully and wonderfully made about sums it up. We were made with both potentials operating within us; the ability to create fear, and the capacity to generate wonder. Furthermore, though we were made with both capacities, "Wonderful are your works," sets a clear direction for which path we are supposed to be pursuing. With that in mind, why do I create so much fear in the hearts of the people I love? Or even the people I meet? What could I do to inspire a greater sense of wonder instead?

Oh, we can call it anger, frustration, disappointment, or any of a number of negative words, but what we create in others is fear. Think of the things that you do or say that cause others to feel poorly toward you. I mention the "do" as opposed to "say", because our non-verbal communications in human interaction make up about 64% of what people understand from us. My mother used to point out to me that when I was exasperated, I would blow out through my nose to signal my displeasure. Many of us fold our arms, roll our eyes, turn away, or become physically flushed. Regardless of whether it is said or shown, our reactions to what any one does are on display for them to read, interpret or misinterpret. Carl Buehner is attributed with saying, "*They may forget what you said, but they will never forget how you made them feel.*" In reality, I make people feel lousy, and sometimes you do to.

In all its forms, including pettiness, arrogance and comparison; judgment may be the single great offender when it comes to creating brokenness in others. We all judge. I think that we should stop calling the pastime of casually observing the folks around us as people watching, and instead refer to it properly as people judging. The people we interact with are constantly coming before the bench of our judgment, in the court of our public opinion.

Judging is a modified version of a thumbs up or thumbs down on everything said, done, worn, or engaged in with the added value of an intensity meter. If someone actually cares about your opinion, and we all do, many are watching for reactions to themselves in your eyes. You may have tremendous power in that moment that you can use judiciously or carelessly. On the negative side, you can create the fear of disappointment not just in the moment, but an image of a possible ongoing disappointment that your child, parent, friend, or acquaintance will not be able to come back from. On the other side, a judgment of pleasure or positivity is just the reward someone may be looking for to encourage them to continue their behavior in security and greater boldness.

"...but no human being can tame the tongue. It is a restless evil, full of deadly poison."

James 3:8 (ESV)

When I judge someone, and they accept or receive my judgment and cross the threshold to action, I have broken off something from them. I have broken off their individuality, their ability to operate as they would like without the weight of my opinion, and their ability to not conform. In this case, I may not have created a sharp edge, but instead blunted or muted something that might better have been left in its original state.

We break off pieces of our children as we mold them into what we believe that they should be. We discourage and judge their behaviors, friends and choices in such a way as to guide them to what we believe to be a better future of more acceptable behaviors, friends and choices. Self-righteously, we point to this passage from the Old Testament to remind us that what we are doing is part of God's plan.

> "Train up a child in the way he should go;
> even when he is old he will not depart from it."
>
> **Proverbs 22:6 (ESV)**

Out of these things and more, we create brokenness in others. It is no small irony that the same issues, if done by someone else, create brokenness in us as well.

> "For I do not understand my own actions. For I do not do what I want, but I do the very thing I hate. Now if I do what I do not want, I agree with the law, that it is good. So now it is no longer I who do it, but sin that dwells within me. For I know that nothing good dwells in me, that is, in my flesh. For I have the desire to do what is right, but not the ability to carry it out. For I do not do the good I want, but the evil I do not want is what I keep on doing. Now if I do what I do not want, it is no longer I who do it, but sin that dwells within me."
>
> **Romans 7: 15-20 (ESV)**

When sharp edges hit soft places in others, it hurts them, and vice versa; but when those same edges hit each other. . . look out!

What do we do about our own brokenness?

We cope with our own brokenness often in broken ways. In addition to revenge or active behaviors of response to what has impacted us, we seek other unhealthy ways to be healed on our own. Masks and disguises for our pain and confusion include humor, sarcasm, and withdrawal. To dampen or diminish our condition, we may turn to addiction or busyness as a distraction. Possibly, with a sense of great nobility, we pour ourselves into helping others or participating in efforts to bind up the broken. We often only realize in helping others that the shards inside and outside ourselves are still very real and very sharp.

The two great challenges of grace are to be completely blessed by it, and secondly, to share it with others. It is challenging, as pointed out in previous chapters, for us to accept and enjoy the grace of God. But, it is equally challenging for us to give that gift away to others. Even though we can never run out of grace that we give away, we are reluctant to share it with others. Why? BECAUSE THEY DON'T DESERVE IT!

This is Satan's greatest weapon! He is thrilled when we accuse of others of unworthiness, because then we are like him. He is the great accuser and the Father of lies. His fall from heaven was due to his belief that mankind was not worthy to be of importance to God, let alone grace when we fell short of His perfection. In short, Satan saw the plan of God, including grace, the redemption through Jesus and the salvation it gained us and said, "NO, they don't deserve it!"

Isn't it ironic that the only way to truly heal our brokenness is to help heal the brokenness in others? The Prayer of St. Francis of Assisi provides a more complete prescription than any words I could find:

> Lord, make me an instrument of your peace:
> where there is hatred, let me sow love;
> where there is injury, pardon;
> where there is doubt, faith;
> where there is despair, hope;
> where there is darkness, light;

where there is sadness, joy.

O divine Master, grant that I may not so much seek

to be consoled as to console,

to be understood as to understand,

to be loved as to love.

For it is in giving that we receive,

it is in pardoning that we are pardoned,

and it is in dying that we are born to eternal life.

Amen.

My brokenness I own. I no longer consider myself to be
the byproduct of dysfunction or circumstance. Rather, I
acknowledge that I have had the freedom of will and choice
throughout my life, and the brokenness I have created in others
and created or allowed to be created in me are of my choosing.
But I do not own me, God does. I just own the brokenness. As I
look in the mirror, I have a lot of questions, and I can make a lot
of lists about my past, or even my today:

Where have I sown hatred instead of love?

Where have I injured?

Where do I doubt and create doubt in others?

When do I despair or cause others to?

When am I the source of sadness?

When do I seek consolation instead of consoling those that need it more?

When do I fail to listen or even attempt to understand?

In short, I can seek forgiveness for my past from the people I have hurt, but I must stop breaking people starting now and going forward. It sounds noble . . .along the same lines as 'and sin no more.' But who am I kidding? This being like Jesus thing is too heavy of a burden for me as a mere mortal to carry. I know me, and this level of decency is way above my ability. I cannot do this on my own, and I am not sure how to even ask God for His help on this one.

What does God do about our brokenness?

First, He would like it to cause us to come to Him. God knows we cannot do this alone. Furthermore, He knows that our efforts to make ourselves better will only frustrate us and discourage us if they don't include Him. However, He has always promised to change us as we come closer to Him.

"And I will give you a new heart, and a new spirit I will put within you. And I will remove the heart of stone from your flesh and give you a heart of flesh.
And I will put my Spirit within you, and cause you to walk in my statutes and be careful to obey my rules."

Ezekiel 36-26-27 (ESV)

"Behold, I am doing a new thing; now it springs forth, do you not perceive it? I will make a way in the wilderness and rivers in the desert."

Isaiah 43:19 (ESV)

Second, testimonies are founded on brokenness; how others have broken us, how we have broken others, how we have broken ourselves, and depending on where we are at in our story, how God and others have helped put us back together. If we are truly to share the good news of redemption and salvation, it begins from the pain of sin and brokenness that we have been redeemed from. Our evangelism is most effective when we are telling a rescue story . . . our story.

"For we are glad when we are weak, and you are strong. Your restoration is what we pray for."

2 Corinthians 13:9 (ESV)

Most importantly, God heals us. Over time, through things appearing as coincidence, the people He puts in our lives and the changes that occur in us in response to His word and teaching, He heals us. God has never desired for us to stay in a condition of brokenness. He has always desired that we were healed unto Him.

"Your righteousness, O God,

reaches the high heavens.

You who have done great things,

O God, who is like you?

You who have made me see many troubles and

calamities

will revive me again;

from the depths of the earth

you will bring me up again.

You will increase my greatness

and comfort me again."

Psalms 71: 19-21 (ESV)

"Come and hear, all you who fear God,

and I will tell what He has done for my soul.

I cried to Him with my mouth,

and high praise was on my tongue.

If I had cherished iniquity in my heart,

the Lord would not have listened.

But truly God has listened;

He has attended to the voice of my prayer.

Blessed be God,

because He has not rejected my prayer

or removed His steadfast love from me!"

Psalm 66:16-20

Brokenness is not easily fixed, which is why it takes God to handle it! Sometimes pieces break off that can be glued back together, sometimes the best we can hope for is for is to soften the edges. Regardless, our brokenness has a purpose which is to be healed in Him.

Chapter 12 Summary

Key Points:

- Each of us is broken in some way as a result of sin, but also in response to the sin that exists in others.
- Brokenness is a means of receiving grace, and also of giving grace to others.
- God is using our brokenness to bring us back to Him, and through us, to bring others to Him as well.

Key Questions:

- What brokenness exists in your life?
- What brokenness do you see in others, and is there someone or many that you have not given grace to because they are unworthy of it from you?
- How can you use your brokenness to share the message of redemption with the people you know?

Prayer:

Father, we are broken, sharp and ugly things that are self-willed and struggle in our sinfulness. We know that we are undeserving of your grace, and yet you give it to us as a never-ending wellspring of your goodness. We ask that we become

Jesus to the people around us and be an example of grace that is shared in abundance. May your Holy Spirit pour out of us to heal the wounds created by ourselves, others, and the nature of sin; so that your glory may be seen and draw more people to you. We are your children, and we bravely ask this in the name of our Lord and Savior, your Son, Jesus . . .the Christ! Amen

Final Thoughts

To me, I considered grace to be so big, that it felt like a target that anyone could not help but hit if they just closed their eyes with the bow and arrow and let fly a shaft. But grace is also unbelievably complex in execution and nuanced in how I work through it every day. Am I forgiving easily, loving naturally, sharing without judgment, and being Jesus to the people I meet? These are the simple questions for me related to whether grace has taken a hold of my being. But, it is a tangle! God does grace like He does everything . . . gracefully! He wants us to make being grace filled and grace sharing so natural that they are non-events in our lives, because that attitude and understanding has become our lives. Unfortunately, we are not God, and not even close to being anything like Him; so we make a jumble out of even the most basic concepts!

It is pretty simple to see what gets in the way of our acceptance and sharing of grace . . . you see the problem every day in the mirror! It is you, or me, or us. We are what keeps us from God and from His grace. The notion that we could set aside justice and mercy, and instead truly love without judgment is something I hear from the pulpit all the time, but in my back pew, I can become skeptical. But the joy of God's love is not just in receiving it, it truly comes from sharing it. If selfishly, I want to feel His love completely, and experience the real joy that comes with that love, I have to get over myself and my goofy preconceived notions and share it unequivocally.

My brother often reminds me that "People can act their way to a new way of thinking, but they cannot think their way to a new way of acting." If we want to receive and give all the grace we can, we have to get started! I get to start with one of my favorite people . . . me! I must accept wholeheartedly and without reservation, the forgiveness and salvation that Jesus won for me, and forget all of my "yes buts" that keep me from really getting it. If my heart cannot fill with grace, how can it possibly overflow with that grace to fill others' hearts? Once I have removed the obstacles to grace that have preceded this conclusion, as well as the many others that stand in my way, I am ready to share that grace.

In many places, I have pointed to the challenges of sharing grace because of our inherent need to be better than others or to be able to claim supremacy in an area of our lives. We know that Jesus is our model, and that as the servant-King, He wants us to not declare our superiority, but instead to be servants to all as if they were superior to us. This level of humility requires so much of our fragile egos, that God had to send the Holy Spirit to dwell within us so we could have the strength to even attempt it. That's right, our ally in sharing this grace is the Holy Spirit, and His indwelling makes it possible to live the life we have been asked to live.

My prayer for you is the same as my prayer for myself:

"Lord, your grace is such an amazing gift that I cannot take it all in, but I sometimes don't want to share it either. I desperately seek your help through your Holy Spirit in being both a servant to those around me, but also to showing them even a portion of the grace you have shown me. Where I am weak, you are strong, so I confidently ask for your help, knowing that you will never abandon this prayer. In your Son's name, Amen."

Made in the USA
Middletown, DE
07 January 2019